GOLD BENEATH THE WAVES

TREASURE HUNTING

THE SURF AND SAND

JIM BROUWER

To My Daughter, Ariana

Acknowledgments

I need to thank so many folks for their help, input, and inspiration.

Thanks to my only and bestest daughter, Ariana, for all her support and help with the graphs, diagrams, and book cover.

Thanks to my detecting buddy, Vince Aluise, for the healthy competition on the beach and for sharing his vast knowledge of fossils and sharks teeth.

A special thanks goes to my friend, Phil Alexander, owner of Common Cents Metal Detectors, for all his valuable insights and metal detecting stories.

Thanks also to my friend, Jason Reep, who has shared his detector information and also his stories of detecting the beach.

Thanks to Don Lewis, mystery writer and good friend, who inspired me to keep moving forward and stay focused.

Thanks also to Rick Poole for his Hurricane Irene finds picture.

Thanks to Dwain Patrick for his photography help and brainstorming on detecting.

Thanks to Ron Guinazzo for his pictures and info about sifting.

I also must thank all the great folks on the Surf and Sand forum at www.thetreasuredepot.com for their support and inspiration. Many of these people I have never met and yet I feel like I know them.

Thanks to Diana Boyce for all her encouragement.

Disclaimer

At some point, while metal detecting, you will get hurt. I'm not saying this to discourage you, only to be honest. You will hurt your back, strain a muscle, or cut your foot on a sharp shell or metal object. Lifting a scoop full of wet sand, over and over again, is hard physical labor!

Cans corrode and will have sharp edges. I despise those fishing weights with the wires that are supposed to 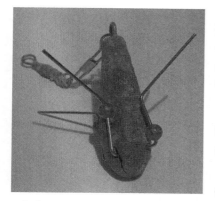 keep the fishing weight in place on the bottom. These are extremely dangerous, an accident waiting to happen. These should be outlawed.

Sparkler wires and stainless steel fish hooks are also out there in the sand.

One of the more insidious things I've run across while surf hunting are pieces of chaise lounge chairs. The ends of the metal tubing corrode and have very sharp jagged edges.

If you surf hunt sooner or later you will be knocked down by a large wave or have the headphones knocked off your head. There are rip currents out there.

At times, the surf will be full of stinging jellyfish.

The beach is a good place to die from sunstroke or hypothermia. Sand blowing off the top of the beach will fill your eyes with grit.

Thunderstorms get my attention and have me heading for the car. You only have to have your hair stand up once to realize that you are very close to becoming a smoldering black spot on the sand. Get the hell out of the water and off the beach when storms approach!

Night hunting is great in the summer but think about where you are. Do not hunt very dark (no motel lights) beaches on moonless nights. Hunt with a friend. Do not become a victim.

Most of the above is common sense. And yet, the lure of gold will override your caution. Golfers use the term risk/reward. This refers to taking a chance. Usually this results in a double bogey. Taking a chance, while metal detecting, can result in losing your life or being hurt.

I am in this for the long term and I hope you are too.

Contents

Introduction...Finding Gold is not Luck

On October 1st of 2006 I moved to Myrtle Beach to find gold and platinum rings. I hunt almost every day and sometimes I will hunt both low tides. Call it an addiction, an obsession, whatever. I am hooked. I need my fix.

Over the past twelve years I've dug a huge number of holes in the sand looking for treasure, most of it at Myrtle Beach. A conservative guess, based on targets retrieved per day hunted, is something close to 100,000 holes.

In 2006 I averaged one gold ring per week.

In June of 2008, I found 22 gold rings. Not only did the number of rings found in 2008 skyrocket but the number of "trophy" rings took a giant leap. I finished 2008 with 117 gold rings. I also found gold chains, pendants, bracelets and gold teeth. My best find in 2008 was an 18K gold chain with a bezel that contained a 1911 five dollar gold coin. Without fully realizing it I had developed a system for finding beach gold.

Finding gold is not luck. Early in my beach hunting career I kept a notebook of my days hunted and my gold ring finds. I did what 90% of the beach hunters do. I went to the beach, turned on the machine, and then swung until my arm fell off. I would look back and there it would be, lying on the sand, twitching. I was successful 10% of the time with this approach. That is a huge amount of effort for very little gold.

Keep doing what you're doing and you'll keep getting what you're getting.   Anon

I needed a better approach. With good equipment and knowledge of wind, waves, and sand you can do better, much better.

Don't get me wrong. Metal detecting the beach/surf is hard work. It is physically demanding and it takes place in a harsh environment. And there will be many days of failure. The beach is not a jewelry store. Successful beach/surf hunters hunt hard and **EARN** every gold ring. But they also hunt smart.

This book will help you find more gold...if you put in the effort. Gold rings are not found on the couch in your living room while watching "Gunsmoke" reruns.

The gold is there to find, but it is up to you to make it happen. You create your own opportunities. You are responsible for your own success.

I hope my Search will never end
For it is deeper than the sand
It is a way of life
A dance on the beach
In the wind and waves and sun
It is the rhythm, the heartbeat of swells
The shout of crashing seas
The whispers of the moon and the night
A lone hunters search
For a softening sky and dawn
Touching the world at first light
Breathing with lungs that inhale the moment
The treasure is
A hunt that will never end

Pelicans

It's all about sand...and shells and rocks and tides and wind and waves and green coins and gold rings and the beatings and dancing hippos and pelicans.

Five heavy brown pelicans approach from the south, gliding down the trough between the waves, soaring without a wing beat, inches above the sea, capturing the wind beneath their large wings and riding free. What propels them forward? How is it possible for these ungainly looking birds to fly for miles without effort? What if we were as efficient as pelicans?

Eagles and hawks and many other birds soar on updrafts, but the only birds I've ever seen fly in the wave troughs are the long strings of pelicans. They have adapted, they have learned the secret. As they fly from place to place they smile, their huge fish holding beaks turned up at the ends, for they feel superior.

Pelicans mock jets and planes that burn thousands of gallons of fuel to move about the sky. Pelicans use a form of trickery, levitation perhaps, which harnesses the natural energy in the bottom of the swells.

Only on certain days do the pelicans display their genius of ocean flight for if conditions aren't favorable, the ocean is flat or choppy, they are only as good as any other bird. Conditions must be favorable.

Metal detecting the beach and surf makes us like the pelicans. If conditions are right, if there is erosion on the beach or a hole in the surf our metal detectors will find the gold. If the beach is sanded-in we will find pull tabs and bottle caps and dimes.

Each day the beach changes, giving us a new face to look at and we must adapt, we must learn the secrets to find the gold. If only we could ride the winds of change on the wings of pelicans.

Ever Shot Yourself in the Foot?..Equipment

The following is a post that I put on the Surf and Sand forum. The title was **You ever shoot yourself in the foot and then stabbed yourself in the eye with a stick?**

Date: Friday, 4 September 2009, at 4:16 p.m.

Got out today and started where I left off yesterday, on the top 1/3 of the beach digging coins and gridding fairly tight. I noticed a detectorist a ways down swinging but not digging. I didn't think too much of it. When he got fairly close he finally dug a target. He had one of those small, foot long, bird cage scoops. It took him forever to dig that target.

Well, we got to talking and he said he was George from Abingdon, VA. I asked him what he had just dug. He said a nail, and he pulls out this big nail.

He was swinging a Sov (Minelab Sovereign) and I was real puzzled how he dug a nail. I asked him if he minded whether I took a look at how he had his Sov set up. He was running all metal, almost no sensitivity, notch out almost everything, discriminate almost everything and his volume at about half.

I started spinning dials and pretty soon had him set up like I had my Sov set up.

We talked a bit more and he said he had never had anyone help him set up his detector.

He turned, took about five steps and gets a signal. His face lights up. He takes out a scoop of sand and shakes it, nothing. Then he repeats the scoop and shake, nothing. Then he moves over one way and scoops. Then he moves over the other way. It was getting embarrassing watching this poor man who obviously couldn't pinpoint a beer can. At last he is shaking the little scoop and I notice a glint of gold. My stomach is turning over. It can't be. No way. Absolutely no way in hell. It has to be an earring or a piece of junk jewelry. All the sand is gone and I step closer. George holds the scoop for me to look in. I am looking into the tunnel. There sits a gold wedding band. It can't be. There is no way.

He pulls it out and holds it. Finally he hands it to me. I heft it and it feels like about 7 grams. I just shake my head and smile.

After George goes down the beach I try to analyze what has happened. I just took a guy that was finding only big nails and gave him the wherewithal to tear up the beach. His first target is a gold wedding band. I try to calculate the odds of this happening. I come up with one gillion to one.

I try to say a prayer, "Dear Lord, That was very nice to give George that gold wedding band. He is on vacation and I am sure this will be the highlight of his vacation. It was also nice to reiterate the fact of beginners luck. You sure were nice to George. You know, maybe someday you might want to spread some of that niceness to someone that is on the Ring Daddy page. Someone that works real hard at detecting. Someone that burns up or freezes to death on the beach daily. Someone that has a beach that was renourished. Someone living at Myrtle Beach. Someone that helps other detectorist set up their detectors. Oh well, you know best. Amen."

A light-yellow butterfly flew by. It is the annual light-yellow butterfly invasion at Myrtle Beach. Within a few days there will be hundreds of yellow butterflies littering the sky, a confetti of yellow wings.

I didn't find any gold today...but it was still a good day...a real good day.

Detectors

Equipment is a big part of hunting the surf/beach. However, swinging a good detector is only half of the two piece puzzle. The other half is the knowledge of how to get the most out of the detector.

What is a good detector for the surf/beach?

Almost any detector will work in the soft sand at the top of the beach. That $150 detector will do fine up there.

Most detectors, especially cheaper detectors, do not work well in the damp beach/saltwater environment. Most will chatter like little old ladies at a quilting bee. You will be hard pressed to distinguish a target from the thousands of false signals. A very poor solution to this chatter is to turn down the sensitivity until the detector is less chattersome. Of course, doing so will limit the depth at which one can find targets. Any target beyond a few inches will not be heard.

Some of the better land detectors can be coaxed into finding targets at fair depth on the beach.

While staying at Apache Campground I kept running into Jim, a detectorist from south of Charlotte. He was swinging one of the better Fisher land detectors. Myrtle Beach was badly sanded-in so we decided to take a trip to Surf City, NC.

We found a very distinct coin line just south of the Surf City pier about two-thirds of the way up from the low tide line. The coin line was no more than three feet wide. If we got above or below that three foot wide strip we found nothing. Not only were the coins lined up they were also layered; buried at 10" to 12" in depth. I was using the Minelab Sovereign and was a digging fool. I noticed that Jim was also digging targets but at a much slower rate. At one point he came over and asked me what I was listening to. I found a target, a nice clear signal, and handed him the headphones. After hearing the signal he said, "No wonder you're tearing it up."

He ended up with 35 coins and I ended up with 103 coins and a broken piece of 10K class ring. I had the better detector for finding coins at this depth in the beach environment. The Fisher land detector might well beat up the Minelab at inland dirt hunting for relics and coins.

One mistake, well not exactly one mistake, which I made when I was began metal detecting was to buy a cheap detector, then a little better detector, and so on until at last I had a real beach detector. I also had a garage full of detectors. This is a very expensive route to getting a good detector. Wives don't like detectors that take up space and don't get used.

The best route to treasure hunting success is to learn as much as possible about a detector before your purchase.

Ask the guys and gals on the metal detecting forums. These people have made the mistakes and are more than happy to share their years of knowledge.

When I emailed my friend, Phil Alexander, in Shallotte, NC about his early metal detecting experience he replied:

> A friend at work bought a metal detector kit for about $15 from the back of a mag. It was junk, but fascinating. I bought a fully assembled Treasure Mate for $13. Hot damn it worked much better, it didn't have to use a transistor radio tuned to a spot without a station to work. It drifted so badly you had to keep your thumb on the tuning wheel, but it worked. My friend, Bob, and I searched on and off for a year and never found a coin, just old shovel heads, old ax heads, oil cans, iron junk. But one glorious day we saw a penny that was lying on the dirt. Bob had a brain storm; "Let's hear what it sounds like." About five minutes later we arrived at the old swimming area out in the woods. That day I started my record of what I found, 72 cents and big class ring. YELLOW GOLD! in the ground. I haven't been fully sane since.

Today's better detectors are light years ahead of the Treasure Mate that Phil used.

First, let me say that I will never cut down someone else's detector. I've seen too many good finds with detectors that were, uh um, not quality detectors.

I like Minelab products. They do an excellent job on the beach and in the surf. The Minelab Excaliber is waterproof and what I use in the surf. I also have a Minelab Sovereign for the beach. However, Minelab is not the only game in town.

The Fisher CZ-20 and CZ-21 both have a good reputation.

Jason in Tennessee often comes down to the MB area to hunt and he uses the Aquasound, a high quality TR (transmitter/receiver) machine and does exceptionally well.

Phil from Ohio comes to MB for a week or two every year and he does very well with a Whites DFX and a Beach Hunter ID. I attribute his success to his knowledge of how to get the most out of his machines.

Whites Dual Field PI is also high on the list of great detectors for the *surf*.

PI's, pulse induction machines, also have some followers and with good reason. PI's will go deep! The disadvantage to a PI is that they do not, for the most part, discriminate iron. This means digging lots of junk on the beach. The surf is a different place than the beach in that it holds far fewer junk targets. Rarely do I find pull tabs and bottle caps in the surf.

I have a Goldquest PI that I have used extensively on the beach at Myrtle Beach. I can not tell you how many bottle caps I have dug at 20". This requires a strong back, a weak mind, and too much patience for most people. I have also dug a couple of average size gold rings beyond 15", a depth that I have never found a gold ring with my Minelab. The Goldquest is not the machine to use on a trash loaded beach.

I recommend buying your detector from a local dealer rather than from a warehouse. A local dealer, face to face, will take the time to show you how to set up your machine and answer the hundred or so questions you have.

Rev Up that Detector!

The other half of the two piece puzzle is the knowledge to get the most out of your detector. Experience is the key to this second part.

Once you have made your choice of an excellent detector you need to get intimate with your detector. Take it to bed.

Read the manual!!

There are some excellent videos online to help learn the functions of your particular machine. I found this video on the Sovereign GT and highly recommend it. http://www.mlotv.com/view/843/the-sovereign-gt-demystified/

Get someone to help you set up the detector. In the story at the beginning of this chapter George admitted he did not have anyone help him with his detector. Many hours of fruitless searching could have been eliminated if he would have had some help upfront.

Phil Alexander has a coin garden, coins and items buried at various depths in his yard. This is an invaluable tool to check out various settings and get the absolute most out of your detector.

Will a larger coil give a better signal on a deep quarter or will a smaller coil work better because there is less iron under the coil? Will opening up iron mask give a better response? Will changing the audio setting or "deep" setting give a better signal? Will a faster or slower swing work better? What about using a different channel? How does "all metal" or "pinpoint" work? Is it possible to get a coin response if a nail is buried next to the coin? How will interference affect the machine? What if the ground is wet vs. dry? What if your hearing is poor in the upper ranges? Is there a way to adjust the tones so that you won't miss signals?

An hour spent making a coin garden, burying coins and a gold ring or two at different depths will give you a lot of answers to those questions. A few hours of testing a detector in a coin garden is worth a hundred days of swinging.

Remember to dig up the gold rings when you move.

The next step to revving up your detector is knowing what it will do in the saltwater/surf environment. Tie a string to a small gold ring and bury it in the wet sand on the beach. Don't use a granny knot. Play with the sensitivity. Try "all metal". Swing fast, swing slow. Test and tweak. Find some black sand, bury the ring, and test some more.

The surf is an even more challenging place to detect. How do waves affect the detector? Is the bottom uneven? Does skimming the bottom give a false? Does raising the coil at the end of the swing cause a false? Does the detector false in ankle-deep water but become stable in deeper water? Find a deep target (a wisp of a signal) and play with the sensitivity. Switch to "all metal".

Learn your machine and get the gold rings that others miss.

You don't want to hear this. If you are a serious detectorist you need a backup machine. A backup machine is like having a new roll of toilet paper within reach when you need it. Metal detector companies often take over a month to fix a faulty machine. Of course, for Foiled Again Jim, that month would be the month that the tropical storm takes all the sand off the beach or a nor'easter finally shows up or a hundred holes show up in the surf.

Ergonomics

When you pull your detector out of the box it most likely will be a very ugly machine when it comes to comfort. Swinging a coil for four hours is hard but if the detector is not set up properly, it will be impossible. In fact, it will cause you much pain. I'm not big on pain and suffering. If you leave the beach early because your rotor cuff no longer rotors you need to think about modifying your detector.

I hip mount the Minelab Sovereign control box in an army surplus ammo bag on a web belt. This takes all the weight off the shaft. This is the most important modification you can make to a detector; *get the weight off the shaft*!

A coil that is too heavy or thick (drags through the water) does two things. It causes fatigue quicker and slows swing speed which leads to less gold rings at the end of the year. The relatively new Minelab 10" Tornado coil is much lighter and thinner than its predecessor. There are many other coils to choose from. Some are very light but I feel like they cross over the line when it comes to structural strength. I need a coil that will hold up to being used 300 days per year.

Some high dollar detectors have the angle of the handle wrong. This puts too much weight on the wrist and makes it extremely uncomfortable to swing. It amazes me that a major manufacturer can build detectors for twenty-five years and still not get this correct.

The Minelab Excaliber has to be the most modified detector on the face of the planet. I never see one on the beach that has not had something done to it. The list of modifications for this detector is impressive.

1. The shaft is replaced with a straight shaft or a long shaft. The long shaft puts the weight of the controls and battery behind the elbow and offsets the weight of the coil.

2. Waterproof connectors will be put on the coil cable to allow changing coils.

3. Hip mount, back mount, or chest mount harnesses are common to get the weight off the shaft. The cables need to be reinforced or they will break.

4. Recently, I saw an Excaliber with a button on the handle to change from "discrimination" to "all metal" mode.

5. The adjustment knobs get replaced with knobs with set screws.

6. Headphones are often replaced with better quality headphones.

One modification that I would like to see is running the coil cable inside the shaft to eliminate drag in the water.

I guarantee it; If you buy an Excaliber, it will get modified.

Headphones

If you don't hear the signals you won't get the gold. A good quality set of headphones is just as important as your detector and your scoop. I use Gray Ghost headphones on my Sovereign. Phil Alexander uses Jolly Roger headphones. Many surf hunters trade out the factory headphones on their waterproof detectors for the waterproof Gray Ghost.

The cable on my Gray Ghost headphones finally broke after many years of extreme use. I went to Wal-Mart and got some Sony headphones for $20 (you also need a ¼" to ⅛"adaptor). These are worthless because the ear muffs do not cover the ears, so they don't block out the wind and wave noise. Being dissatisfied with the Sony's I ran to a pawn shop and picked up an old set of Whites headphones. These were comfortable and blocked out the outside noise but did not have a limiter on them. The limiter keeps sounds from busting your eardrums. The Whites are now my emergency backup headphones.

I recently ran into a guy that loved his Black Widow headphones more than his retired Gray Ghost headphones.

Clive Clynick, who has written many books on detecting, recommends Mr. Gold Master headphones.

Top quality headphones are worth every penny.

Coils

It was a day filled with targets. I'd found a large hole in the surf out in front of the Landmark. Using my small 7¼" coil I thought that I had a solid target approximately two feet in diameter. I kept swinging, messing with the edge of that target and realized that there was a coin along one edge. I dug it and found two coins in the scoop. Then I picked out another coin with the small coil and dug it. I kept nibbling away at the solid target, coin by coin, until the area was quiet. A big coil would have made separation of the targets almost impossible. A small coil excels when there are lots of targets.

Thomas Dankowski wrote a very interesting article called, "Coil Myths." Basically, it stated that a coil looks at soil *volume*. An 8" coil looks at approximately one gallon of soil while an 11" coil looks at approximately seven gallons of soil. Seven times as much!! There is seven times the mineralization under the 11" coil as the 8" coil. Therefore, an 8" coil may have greater depth than the 11" coil due to mineralization.

Small Coils vs Big Coils

Small coils:

• Excel when there are lots of targets, making separation and identification of targets much easier.
• Often will go just as deep as big coils.
• Are easier to swing.
• Pinpoint much easier than large coils.
• Will find smaller objects.
• Can be put in the hole to isolate the signal.
• Cover much less volume.

Big Coils:

• Cover much more volume. This is a huge advantage on the beach...and in the surf if targets are spread out.
• Will go deeper where mineralization is minimal.

• Heavier and harder to swing, causing early fatigue.
•Often not as stable as a small coil.

On days when the waves are too big or the current too strong to detect the surf and you find yourself up on the beach the big coil is a huge advantage, covering a lot more surface area per swing. Charlie Smith and Phil Alexander are both using the 10x12 SEF coil with their Sov's with impressive results. Charlie uses a "swingy thingy" (bungee cord support) to help carry the weight of the coil.

When I used a very large coil, the WOT 15" coil, I had to turn down my sensitivity to make it run stable. However, I still believe a large coil will see more targets on the beach because of the larger surface area. From years of swinging on the beach I recommend a 10"-12" coil.

Do not use the coil cover! It will cause you much heartache. Sand and water will get between the coil and the coil cover, move around, and drive you nuts with falsing.

 Instead, mix up a batch of marine epoxy and coat the bottom. To make the job aesthetically pleasing take a piece of masking tape and tape around the outside edge leaving a ⅛" lip above the bottom. This will act as a dam for the epoxy. Another advantage to the epoxy bottom is that it shows you where the coil is wearing out.

Another option is to spray the bottom of the coil with truck bed liner. This is much easier to apply, however if the coil takes a lot of abuse, banging into rocks, and you want to apply epoxy later I would think that you would need to remove the layer of truck bed liner from the coil to get good adhesion.

Scoops

My friend, Phil Alexander of Shallotte, NC, being the mechanical engineer minded fellow that he is, built his first water scoop using a broom handle, a Folgers coffee can and a nail. He says that he actually recovered some targets with this scoop. I guess anything is possible. Plans to build this scoop are available for $19.95.

If you detect the surf you need a hugely sturdy water scoop that will take out a lot material quickly. Stainless steel scoops designed for the surf are heavy. The advantage of stainless steel over aluminum is that the lip is much thinner making digging easier. The main disadvantage of stainless steel is the weight. Another disadvantage of a stainless steel scoop is that the lip is thin and when it bangs into your shins or Achilles tendon it will cut you. Then the sharks will come. A good surf scoop will run $150-$200, a sizeable but necessary investment.

I presently own a stainless steel Sunspot Stealth scoop. This is my second Sunspot scoop; I wore the first one out. I like the design of the new scoop better. It seems sturdier and the hole number and placement seem better. I also like the fact that I can replace the wood handle with a handle from a home improvement warehouse for less than six dollars if the handle breaks. I have modified the bottom of the scoop by putting some plastic mesh in the bottom with some cable ties. This is for those small items, like BB's and small pendants that keep falling through the bigger holes.

Now, if I have an object that falls through I simply turn the scoop up as I bring it to the surface. Using this method I am now able to corral these small items.

If one uses a PI detector the list of objects that will drop through the scoop holes gets very long; nails, bobby pins, and tiny bits of iron come to mind. Most PI detectorists attach a strong magnet in the bottom of their scoops to pick up these irritating, aggravating, annoying, misbegotten pieces of junk.

There are now quite a few good surf scoops on the market. Once again, get on the metal detecting forums and find out what people are using.

Bill Babb makes an aluminum scoop that has a stainless steel lip that some detectorists rave about (pro-scoops.com).

Surf scoops are not beach scoops.

Phil Alexander made his own stainless steel beach scoop and as a beach scoop it is superb. It is fairly lightweight, has a small profile, and makes quick work of retrieval. Phil has dug a zillion targets with it on the beach. It is too small for the surf but I doubt that you could find a better thought out design for a beach scoop.

Phil's Homemade Scoop

Stealth Scoop

I've seen many attempts at scoop building and most lack the structural integrity needed for digging and lifting massive amounts of sand and shells.

If one hunts the soft sand upper beach (I never do) one needs a scoop with a wire mesh bottom. A few shakes, the sand is gone and the target is in the bottom. A long handle prevents you from bending over a hundred times per outing and saves your back.

Shovel

A shovel is worthless in the surf. However, there are times when the upper beach has just eroded and pulled the sand down over the lower beach. It is an upper beach day. All of your efforts should be on the upper beach. Here is where a short shovel excels. I have one that I bought years ago and it is perfect for me (my shovel is 40" from tip to the top of the D handle). It is much lighter than my scoop and I have learned to use it with one hand. I push it into the sand

and then lean it back while pulling on it. The sand usually comes out in one large chunk. Then I use the tip of the shovel to pick up my target. Light and fast!

Pouches

I hip mount my Sovereign and a large green Minelab pouch using an army belt.

I use a nail apron when I surf hunt.

A nail apron with two pouches is fine for most metal detecting. One pouch is for gold rings and the other is for platinum rings. If I had a third pouch it would be for gold bullion.

One day out in the surf I dug the same small pendant twice. Check your nail apron for holes.

I ran into Dick Shoemaker the other day and was looking at his Pro Beach and Water Hunting Pouch. It is well made, really nice. I now have pouch envy.

Wetsuit

The winter morning was overcast and gloomy. Earlier I had spotted the hole in the surf from Apache Pier and was now up to my chin in the dark ocean water. This was not a productive hole; no large shells or rocks on the bottom and yet I was getting a few signals, mostly sinkers. I held out hope that somewhere in this deep hole a gold ring would reside. A large wave rolled over my head and knocked my headphones off. I cussed and waited. The day seemed full of one, two punch waves. Another wave rolled over my black neoprene clad skull. I placed the headphones back on my head. This hole was being hateful. It was too deep and I was too buoyant. The wetsuit added to my buoyancy, my weightlessness. I was one of the dancing hippos in Fantasia. When I got a signal I was having a heck of a time putting enough pressure on the scoop to dig. My solution was to set the scoop into place and then holding onto the scoop handle I tried to jump up and down on the scoop. How'd that work? Not too good.

I kept trying to visualize a gold ring in the scoop to keep my spirits up. My spirits were being beat up by the waves.

A string of pelicans glided silently by in the bottom of a wave trough, close enough I could see their eyes, their bodies within an inch or two of the water, sledding on a carpet of air. Riding, riding without effort, at peace with the ocean, the winds, and the waves, alive in the day and going somewhere, in sync and in tune with the music of their home.

I heard the sirens above the detectors threshold sound. The screaming got closer and more obnoxious. A fire truck appeared on the campground road. A beach patrol SUV flew down the beach and stopped.

I was being rescued again by the City of Myrtle Beach. The police officer waved me in.

"Are you alright?" he asked.

"Yeah, I'm fine."

"Uh, we got a call about someone being pulled under the waves."

I hesitated, "Uh, I had a couple of big waves roll over me, that's all."

"Aren't you cold?"

"No, not really."

"How about doing me a favor and not going so deep that you look like you need help?"

At least he didn't tell me to stay out of the water or take me in for questioning.

At Myrtle Beach the surf is uncomfortably cold from November through April, six months of the year. The surf water temperature in the dead of winter is close to 50 degrees. After a few months of using your wetsuit daily you will feel as though you live in the wetsuit.

I have a two piece wetsuit; a 7mm neoprene farmer john and a 7mm neoprene shorty. This gives me 14 mm of neoprene on my upper body. I also have a neoprene hood, boots, and gloves. On warm winter days I am baking potato hot until I get into the water.

If I am in the water for more than an hour I will pee in my wetsuit. This is a body warming experience and usually brings a smile to my face. The wetsuit after a few peeings will get gamey. Don't leave the wetsuit to dry out in your VW. There are cleaning products that scuba places sell just for this problem.

My farmer john wet suit has straps that go over the shoulders and use Velcro® on the front to keep the straps in place. This is poor design. I am a bit long in the torso so the straps are short. After getting the farmer john pulled up the straps hang down my back. I can't quite reach the straps by reaching over my shoulders. If I try to pull the wetsuit up higher to get the straps higher in the back it puts pressure on the privates, a self-inflicted wedgy. The best method I've found is to lean to one side and reach across under my armpit to snag the strap and then pull it over my shoulder. Sometimes this contortion stretches muscles that were never meant to be stretched. A good yoga exercise is to put on a wet suit in a Geo Metro.

Wetsuits have improved a lot since I bought mine and you can probably get by with less neoprene. The new ones also tout that they are more flexible.

A dry suit would be great in January and February but they are holy tomato paste expensive. Someday, when I find the Lost Hope diamond ring I will get a dry suit.

Jason Reep has a neoprene vest (NRS Men's Hydroskin Vest) that he uses during the transition season between warm and cold surf water.

Neoprene adds buoyancy and becomes a problem in chest deep water. A weight belt is used to offset the buoyancy.

Weight Belt

I hate my weight belt and rarely use it. Trudging down the beach in a wetsuit with a twenty-five pound weight belt is cruel and unusual punishment. If I happen to make it to the surf, a fifty/fifty chance, there is always the heart stopping return trip up the beach to the car.

The weight belt does help you dig targets and does help offset the buoyancy in deep water. I just have a hard time justifying the advantage.

It's fairly easy to imagine the big adventure of being knocked down by a large wave with a metal detector in one hand, a long handled scoop in the other and the equivalent of a boat anchor tied around ones middle. I've always been told to stay calm under conditions like this. After a second of staying calm I would probably resort to underwater screaming.

Underwear

This is a personal problem. My thighs rub together and cause thigh rash. Thigh rash is a summer thing; a real problem when it is hot and humid. It feels like there is a rasp used for horseshoeing placed between my thighs. This is very debilitating. On the pain scale it is about a 9.8.

Thigh rash makes me walk bowlegged.

Underwear with the legs that come half way down the thigh solved this problem.

Swim Trunks

I bought some nice shorts with a gob of pockets that had zippers thinking they would be great for detecting in the water. Within a few short weeks the saltwater had corroded the zipper pulls until they fell off.

One day I tried to use running shorts for swim trunks and they captured the air and gave me bubble-butt. Stick with swim trunks.

Your Body

Metal detecting the surf/beach is a physically taxing activity. Swinging a coil is relatively easy until you swing it for four hours. It takes some getting used to.

Digging into heavy wet sand with a scoop or digging a deep hole in the surf can elevate the heart rate. You should know you are capable of doing this type of work. You need to be in at least fair physical condition. If you have heart/lung problems this is not the hobby for you.

Yesterday I was on a stretch of beach that looked interesting to the north. The first little washout had no targets. Then it started to rain. I traipsed to the next washout and got a couple of targets. The rain came harder. It looked better further north. I kept walking and detecting as I went. Now the rain fell in sheets. I finally got to a spot and found two rings, one titanium and one silver. It spurred me on to the north. More rain. More targets and then another silver ring. I was cold and wet. At last, the Minelab Sov gave its wail that lets you know the battery is very low. I turned around and headed for the car. It took close to forty minutes to walk back to the car. I'd walked at least a total of four miles.

No one says you have to walk four miles or dig deep targets. You can go out for an hour and enjoy the day swinging and find a few targets.

If however you are serious about finding as much gold as possible in the surf and on the beach you must realize that this is a physical hobby. Do not underestimate the amount of work involved.

Be kind to your body. Be kind to your back. On the beach do not bend over to pick up your targets! Don't do it!! Take your scoop or your shovel and capture the target and raise it to your other hand. Imagine a day when you find over 150 targets on the beach and you have bent over to retrieve each one. Pain makes us smarter.

Good fuels for the body are complex carbohydrates. Sugar and caffeine will give you a quick burst but will not be with you after three hours. I like a bowl of Grape Nuts and yogurt with raisins before I hit the beach. Take a banana or energy bar.

Make sure you have water to drink on hot days.

Use sunscreen every time you go out.

Protect your eyes from the sun and glare with a pair of polarized sunglasses. Polarized sunglasses are an absolute must for seeing holes in the surf. They also let you see the sharks and jellyfish that you otherwise won't see.

Dress in layers and be prepared for the worst. The beach is a place of wind and changing weather. I have seen times in the summer when I was overly hot and a quick thunderstorm cooled it to the point I was chilled.

The wind coming off the ocean can be bitterly cold in the winter. I sometimes dress like I'm going ice fishing in Siberia. This allows me to keep swinging the beach when others have gone home...or stayed at home. Wimps.

Your Mind

Think positive thoughts. Visualize a nice gold or platinum ring with diamonds. Not everyday will give you a gold ring. Enjoy the pelicans and gulls, the dolphins arcing through the waves, the laughter of a child, the sight of two elderly people holding hands, the smell of the sea, or the sight of a shrimp boat far out to sea. Stay in the moment, to heck with yesterday and tomorrow. Do you know how lucky you are to be where you are today?

Be flexible, open minded. The slate should be clean as you walk out onto the beach. Everyday is different. Some days it is better to hunt the beach than the surf and visa versa. Is that a low spot that wasn't there yesterday? Is that a hole in the surf?

Forums

Today we Google, Tweet, Facebook, and Youtube. And if you are into metal detecting the beach/surf you should be all up in the online metal detecting forums.

Warning: Metal detecting forums are addictive and must be handled with extreme caution. I don't want someone losing their job because they were, uh, "researching" the Ring Daddy Page with the boss standing behind them.

Forums are places to share successes (brag a little bit), failures, and information. Two forums that I recommend joining are www.thetreasuredepot.com and www.findmall.com. Both of these are excellent and for different reasons.

I like the Surf and Sand forum at the Treasure Depot because of the format and friendly folks that show off their finds. Ask a question about beach or surf hunting on this forum and you will get some great advice. I also like the Ring Daddy Page. If you need your eyes to be bugged out and your jaw to drop open the Ring Daddy Page is a great place to visit. This is gold ring porno.

I also like the Beach and Water Detecting forum at the Finds Treasure Forum, but what brings me back to Findmall.com most often is the many forums that cover each detecting subject matter and each type of detector. If you need some specific information about something detecting, you can find it at Findmall.com. The Modifications Forum is a strange and wonderful place. Here, it is possible to find the inventors of the detecting world, tinkering, tweaking, pulling the guts out of a detector and sometimes successfully putting it back together again. The PI Technology Forum is the absolute best forum if you ever think about buying a PI detector.

But wait, there's more. There are forums to buy and sell your detecting gear, forums for bottle hunters, and forums for gold prospecting. I know of no better way to become a metal detecting nerd than to get involved with a forum. It is also a super place to daydream and wile away the hours that you can't be on the beach.

Can't quite figure out how to get your shaft apart that is cemented together by saltwater? Need some help with your detector's settings or for some reason your detector is acting unreasonable? Ask for help on the forums. You will be amazed at how open and willing other detectorists are to share their expertise. They may not share the location where they are finding the gold rings but they will share almost everything else.

Of course, the real benefit of the forums is the knowledge that there are people just like you who share an interest in metal detecting and a drive to learn and get better at it. Members of metal detecting forums share bits and pieces of their lives and in a short period of time many of the folks on the forums seem like old friends. You may never meet them face to face but you know they are good people who love the outdoors and the thrill of seeing gold in their scoops.

The Treasure Vehicle

To really find gold rings on a consistent basis one needs to move around. I detect from Holden Beach in NC to Pawleys Island, SC. Of course, I try to detect as close to home as possible but this is not necessarily where there is some erosion and erosion is key to finding gold rings. One needs to go to where the gold is.

An economical vehicle will make it much less painful when it comes to driving forty miles to detect. Also, your decision making will be less influenced by $4 per gallon gas if your vehicle gets good gas mileage.

Myrtle Beach allows golf carts on streets with speed  limits of 35 mph or less. A friend and detectorist, Dick Shoemaker, has an electric vehicle that has a range of 40 miles that he uses daily when checking out the beach.

Skills

"Jim, how do you retrieve the target with your scoop?" asked Harold.

I had met Harold a couple of days earlier on the beach. I could tell by his tone and demeanor that he was frustrated. I hadn't thought about this skill for a long time. It was second nature to me. I simply found the target and scooped the target.

Harold had the tools, a fine water detector and a nice water scoop, but he lacked the skill to retrieve the target.

I was navel to chest deep in the surf. The waves were bouncing me around and pounding on me but I was in a hole and finding treasure. I turned sideways as another wave came through. This move presents a slightly thinner profile for the wave to pummel. This too is a skill that one learns when one is being beaten on. I found a high sound and set my scoop, dug the ocean bottom, and pulled the scoop off to the side of the hole. I swung the detector across the hole and knew I had the coin in the scoop. I shook the scoop on the way to the surface. As the scoop cleared the water I spotted the quarter in the mess of shells, plucked it from the scoop and held it up for Harold. He shook his head. I could tell that he considered what I had just done something akin to a magician pulling a rabbit from a hat or solving a Rubik's cube in less than a minute.

I swung the detector around and located another coin. "Here's a target. Go ahead and retrieve this one." I backed off so that our detectors wouldn't interfere with each other. Harold located the coin and began digging the bottom. After three attempts with nothing in the scoop I said, "Let me get it." I waded in, located the coin, and had it in the scoop within seconds.

"Let's go up on the beach and practice. This is too hard out here."

On the beach I became the teacher. I threw a coin down on the sand. "OK, we've located the target. We want to get the coil right over the center of the target. I stopped the middle of the coil directly over the center of the coin. Now we move our left foot up to the back of the coil, just touching the coil. We pull the coil away and put the scoop just touching our left foot. We now dig the target. Try it a few times. It feels awkward at first."

Harold moved in and repeated the steps.

"Now, do it with your eyes closed."

Harold smiled, closed his eyes and retrieved the coin.

"Do it a couple more times."

When we got back in the surf Harold located a coin and retrieved it in two scoops. He was grinning. I had created a monster; another target digging, surf hunting fool.

Here are the basic retrieval steps.

1. Locate the coil directly over the center of the target.

2. Place your left foot behind the coil (if you swing the detector with the right arm).

3. Remove the coil and place the scoop just in front of your foot (without cutting off your toes). You are ready to dig.

A skill that is overlooked is the basic swing. The swing should put the coil as close to the sand as possible without making contact for the entire swing. Many detectorists look as though they are chopping weeds. Their swings arc upward at the end of each swing, sometimes to the point that the coil is twenty inches off the sand. If you grid and have a good swing you can feel confident that you have left very little behind.

Twice during the summer of 2008 I had small gold chains fall through my scoop holes just as it reached the surface. I was unable to retrieve either one of these chains. One of the chains made no signal sound and it was exasperating to know that it was right in front of me. I repeatedly scooped hoping it would come to the surface. The other chain made the smallest of low signal sounds and I think my attempts to scoop it were successful but the chain would drop through the scoop holes before it surfaced. It doesn't help that the surf water at Myrtle Beach has no visibility.

We all have small objects fall through the scoop holes; bb sinkers, small pendants, bellybutton thingies, and small gold chains. I found a small 18K gold pendant with a nice diamond on the beach that would have easily fallen through my scoop holes. As noted earlier in the Scoops section, modifying the scoop with plastic mesh and a strong magnet will eliminate losing most small targets.

Lost targets will drive you to the booby hatch. "Where in the heck did that target go?"

It is quite easy to lose a target on the beach or in the surf. Both are maddening.

On the beach, often what has happened is that as you dug you disturbed or moved the target. The dime that was lying flat under the sand is now upright to the coil or it has been shoved up against the hole wall or the little demon is stuck inside your scoop. Most of the time digging out another scoop of sand will bring the target to life. Don't give up on it; dig out another scoop. Very rarely when you have dug with the scoop or shovel you have made contact with the target and shoved it deeper. The remedy is the same; take out another scoop of sand.

After I have my pile of sand out of the hole I swing my coil over the pile and isolate the target. Then I kick the sand sideways to spread out the sand and locate the target. Once in a while, when I kick the pile a coin or ring will stand upright and roll several feet. If you do not happen to see the escapee you will attribute the lost target to alien forces. Look out there three to six feet and you will find it.

In the surf losing a target can get squirrely. Most of the time taking out another scoop of sand works. However, lightweight targets, pull tabs for example, will take flight with the current never to be seen again.

Other Surf Hunting Skills:

• Learn to identify holes in the surf by sight, the movement of the waves, and using your feet to bump large shells and fist sized rocks (the foot test).

• Use the scoop test. At Myrtle Beach I need a treasure indicator in the bottom of my scoop; peat, mud, shells and rocks, or dark charcoal sand. It tells me I am down to the hard layer where the treasure lies. I can only remember one time getting a gold ring in my scoop without a treasure indicator and that was at Sunset Beach. It clanged around as I brought it to the surface. It seemed surreal to see only a gold ring without anything else in the scoop.

• Be super observant of swimmers. Is the surf area (between the low tide line and the sandbar) sanded-in and the swimmers only ankle deep until they reach the sandbar or are they chest deep? Are the swimmers reaching down and picking up conch shells or other big shells? If so, that is where you need to be. Detect the deepest water first.

• Work with the low tide; detect the deepest water at the lowest point of the low tide. Sometimes the surf is an unruly wild child, and the surf is only workable for the hour at the lowest of the tide. Seize the moment.

• Do the scoop flip-flop. Instead of digging with your hands all the way to the bottom of the scoop where the gold ring is, take out the biggest shells and then twist the scoop side to side. As the scoop rolls to the side often the gold ring will reveal itself.

• Do not wear anything metal that may interfere with the detector. Keep the scoop far enough away that it does not interfere with the detector.

• Use buildings or palm trees or anything permanent as markers to help you grid the bottom of the ocean. Pretty girls sitting on the beach are not good markers.

• Know the exact length of your swing so you do not leave gaps or overlap too much.

• Experiment. Does all metal mode give you more depth and more "good" targets? Some of the better detectorists that use the Excaliber use pinpoint (all metal), sensitivity to max and threshold just *inaudible*.

• Turn sideways to an oncoming wave...unless you are wider in that dimension.

• In moderate sized waves, two footers, it is easier to retrieve the target between waves. Let the wave hit you and then quickly set up and retrieve.

• If a mid-tone target keeps crawling away from your scoop, it is a pull tab. They are light and will float out of the scoop. Heavy objects are almost always beneath the shells in the scoop.

• As soon as you know the target is in the scoop begin shaking (not you, the scoop). All of the sand should be out before it reaches the surface.

• After you have retrieved the target from your scoop double check the pile and your hole.

• Also, there are times when the waves are too big or the current is just too powerful and your efficiency to retrieve targets is so impaired you are better off detecting the beach.

"A good man always has to know his limitations." Dirty Harry

Beach Hunting Skills

- Learn to read the beach. You are looking for signs of erosion.
- Do not detect a sanded-in beach. Move! Use Run and Gun (Chapter 12).
- Once a good target is dug, search the immediate vicinity using a spiral pattern, @.
- Desperation Time. As a last resort, when I cannot find an eroded area, I grid up and down to locate a coin line or a level on the beach that is most productive. If I find a productive level on the beach I grid parallel with the low tide line.
- Learn to retrieve quickly. One shovel or scoop retrieves should take no more than thirty seconds including kicking the sand back in the hole. Do not use a handheld pinpointer on the beach. If the item is so small that it requires a pinpointer grab a handful of sand and the item and put it in your pouch. You can deal with it at the house.
- Drag your scoop or shovel so you do not waste time detecting over the same area.
- Grid. Know the swing path of your coil and grid efficiently. If you are gridding correctly the lines in the sand from dragging your scoop should look like an "m".

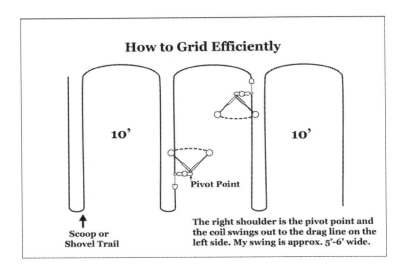

Go Fast, Go Slow!!

I hunt erosion. I dare say that normally 95% of the beach or surf is not eroded.

When I see a hole in the surf or a runnel with rock and big shells I run to it. I don't give a tinkers dam about the rest of the beach or surf. Run Forrest, Run! (my middle name is Forrest). Sprint to the honey hole as quickly as possible.

Now, once I am at the gold hole I slam on the brakes and switch to my lowest, slowest, old man with brown socks gear. This is where I grid slow and shuffle along making sure that I do not miss anything.

Go fast, go slow!

Go with the flow. Enjoy the sunrise, the smell of the sea. Linger in the moment. Watch the gulls and the sandpipers and the dolphins. Carry a story with you for folks that you meet. We hurry too much and miss so much.

The Loss

Valerie walked the shore, leaving shapely foot prints in the wet sand, pushing four little sandpipers up the beach. She recalled the long walks she and her husband used to enjoy, sometimes holding hands, sometimes his arm wrapped around her shoulders and her arm around his waist.

The night air seemed the perfect humidity and temperature. At first the water sloshing up and encircling her feet felt cold but soon it didn't. The lights were on at the pier and she could hear the music of the band at Ocean Annie's Beach Bar. It would be a long walk to Ocean Annie's, but all she had was time.

She paid the lady at the pier store the dollar and walked down the east coasts longest wooden pier. A few fishermen propped their rods with the butt end of the rods under the wooden seats, with the middle of the rod over the rail. The lights illuminated the spider lines that sagged into the darkness. Some of the anglers appeared to be sleeping and Valerie wished it were that easy. She walked until the pier made a T at the end. It was too early in the season for the King Mackerel fishermen and the end of the pier was sleepily quiet. The tired swells drifted through the pilings. She put her elbows on the slanted blood stained rail and looked over the edge. Jellyfish hung suspended just below the ebony and silver surface, small saucer sized blobs and then she spotted a large man-of-war with its long tentacles hanging into the depths. A raven of iridescent blue and black alit on the railing towards the corner. She fiddled with her gold wedding band and looked as far away as she could see. Summer heat lightning, tentacles of light, showed her where the world ended.

"Whatcha thinking about?"

Valerie flinched. An elderly black man stood down the rail with his elbows on the rail just like she had hers. She was sure there had been no one there a few seconds before. She had not heard him come up.

Her mouth quivered, "I'm thinking about God and why things are like they are?"

"I come out here sometimes and think the same things."

She wondered how another persons thought could be the same in the same place. Were the thoughts trapped within the confines of the night and the rails? Valerie looked at the black man and noticed that his skin was the same blue-black as the ravens. She looked to the corner and the raven was gone.

"Sure is quiet," said the black man.

"I used to like quiet but now I need something, I need.........I just need." A tear ran down her face.

"It's not good to stand out here when you're like that."

They both watched the heat lightning wander through the clouds at the edge of the ocean.

"I have to do something. Can you leave me alone for a few minutes?"

"Are you sure you're going to be OK?....You're not going to do something crazy?"

"No, I'll be OK?"

"The pier will be closing in about fifteen minutes." The black man turned and walked quietly down the pier.

Valerie listened and realized the band at Ocean Annie's must be taking a break. She stood amid the quiet and the darkness. There had been far too much of both this past year. She talked slowly to the night, "I hope you understand. I need to go on. I need to laugh again. There's been too much sadness. I don't feel alive anymore. I just need to laugh again.....I will always love you...you know that."

Valerie pulled the gold ring from her finger and kissed it goodbye.

* * * * *

The above story is fiction. I'm not sure, but it might be against the law to put a fiction story in a non-fiction book.

Rings are lost in many ways.

Most rings are lost in the water. The water is cool, the fingers shrink, and the rings fall off.

Some rings are lost by being thrown off while tossing a football or Frisbee or playing volleyball. Some rings are tossed into the ocean after a heated argument between significant others. "Significant others" covers a lot of territory now days. Some rings are also lost by crafty tourists that take their rings off and put them on the beach towel or in their shoes where children running knock them into the sand. Or the afternoon storm suddenly sends a bolt of lightning crackling onto the beach and the tourists grab the kids and towels and run for their lives.

Body surfing is popular at Myrtle Beach. It looks like fun but it is not. The body surfer waits until a large wave arrives and tries to swim fast enough to ride the wave in. At the end of the ride the body surfer is often slammed into the bottom of the ocean. Here is where I believe a lot of gold chains are lost.

Skim boarding is another activity enjoyed by the younger crowd, mostly guys, wanting to hurt themselves. A piece of plywood is thrown down onto a thin layer of water and the skim boarder runs to jump aboard. It requires skill, agility, timing, finesse, and a grand sense of balance. Skim boarders frequently get to see their feet silhouetted against the blue sky. Skin, body parts and class rings are dislocated.

I'm a people watcher and one thing I notice is that women in particular like to move their short chaise lounge chairs close to the surf line and put their hands in the wet sand. Some rings have to be lost this way.

Recently I had a guy ask me if I would look for his wedding ring that he had lost. He had been married five days. He was in the surf with fairly large waves carrying one of those body boards. A wave hit the board in his hand and wrenched the ring off his finger. I looked for his ring for an hour in the surf and did not find it.

I find many more men's rings than women's rings and it seems that I find men's rings lower on the beach or in the water than women's rings.

If high tide is from noon until say three o'clock, when most people are on the beach, then rings will be lost from the top of the beach all the way to the sandbar. If low tide is in the afternoon then most rings will be lost beyond the low tide line. **I believe that more rings are lost in the surf zone** (the area seaward of the low tide line) **than on the beach.**

I've been asked by two different people to help find their lost gold rings in one afternoon on one small stretch of beach. How many gold rings are lost on the Grand Strand in one hot July day?

I always try to help find a lost ring if I can. However, when someone comes up and says they have lost their gold ring and then point out to the ocean I let them know that the chances of finding that ring are very small.

There was a discussion on one of the metal detecting forums about whether people are more careful today with their jewelry, putting it in the motel room vault or just not wearing it on the beach. I still see a lot of jewelry on the beach. People are on vacation and this is a detail that few people think about. They just want to relax and enjoy the sun and the waves.

I doubt that metal detectorists find five percent of all the gold rings lost each year. Every year more rings are added to the carpet of gold beneath the waves.

Where are the Gold Rings?

To find the gold rings we need to know where they reside. Where are they hiding? Almost all of the heavy precious metal items live below the porous sand, atop a solid layer. Just as seniors migrate to Florida or Arizona, gold rings drop through the sand until they hit something solid that stops their vertical descent. The trip through the sand to the solid layer may take minutes or days.

At Myrtle Beach there are over sixty years of gold being dropped on the beaches that are now atop the solid layer.

The depth of the sand over the gold may be zero inches or many feet (far beyond your detectors capabilities).

The only exceptions to this are new drops. They may not have completed their journey to the solid world below. There are only a few days of new drops that have not gotten to the solid layer.

Forget new drops. Banish new drops from your mind. Do not hunt for new drops. I can find the Holy Grail before I can find a newly dropped gold ring.

To find Multiple Gold Rings one needs to find the solid layer beneath the sand.

What is the Solid Layer?

At Myrtle Beach there are four types of solid layers; large shells and rocks, coquina rock, peat, and hardpan. Each one is totally different but they all hold the gold.

Technically, large shells and rocks are not solid...but they are solid enough to keep treasure items from moving deeper. I've seen large shells flip over in the surf so it stands to reason that a ring atop shells might slowly get buried by flipping shells. It has been my experience that when I find a hole in the surf with a large shell/rock base I find gold rings. At Myrtle Beach large shells/rocks is what I run into most often when finding gold rings. Large shells and rocks not only will be in the surf but will sometimes be visible in washout areas or runnels on the beach. *I am always hunting for a low spot with large shells and rocks.*

There are spots; Hurl Park, 2nd Ave Pier, and north of 82nd Ave North that often had coquina rock showing before the renourishment. Now, (2011) they are completely covered with sand.

The area at 73rd Ave North has peat beneath the sand. Now, (2011) there is a shell layer over the top of the peat layer. The new shell layer is due to the renourishment.

At North Myrtle Beach, near Cherry Grove, I've run into hardpan (hard mud) before the renourishment. I have not hunted this area since the 2007-08 renourishment.

Dark Gray Sand Layer

There is also a layer that I run into that puts me on high alert for a gold ring; the dark gray sand layer. If I dig a target and see dark gray sand in my scoop I get excited.

This is extremely fine sand, highly compacted and my guess is that it is highly mineralized. I slow way down in an area of dark gray sand for I know there is a gold ring nearby. Once again, the dark gray sand layer is below the light gray sand layer and only shows up in holes or eroded areas.

• To find Multiple Gold Rings one needs to find the solid layer beneath the sand.

• Solid layers that hold the gold rings are:
Large shells/rocks (conch shells and fist-sized rocks)
Peat
Coquina Rock
Hardpan or Hard Mud
Dark Gray Sand Layer

• Forget new drops!

But Don't Gold Rings Move Around in the Surf?

A lot of research has been done on this subject. Detectorists have done all sorts of elaborate test to determine gold ring movement.

Thomas Dankowski tied a string to a gold ring and had it drop 23" through the sand in five minutes. I tried the same experiment at the low tide line with small waves rolling over the top of my gold ring. After twenty minutes my gold ring was still visible. If you want to look like the supreme dorkaroo stand at the low tide line with a string tied to a gold ring for twenty minutes. At one point, in the experiment, the gold ring was not visible, covered by a thin layer of sand. Then a wave came up and removed most of the sand.

If I had found a sloppy sand area, a place where I would sink to my calves in a few seconds I think my results would have been very different. But not all gold rings are lost in the slop.

• Rings eventually drop through the sand to the hard layer.

Do rings travel up and down the beach like a tourist, sometimes moving miles? Detectorists on the forums that have returned rings sometimes get told that the ring was lost miles from where it was found.

I have a real hard time with this from my experience at Myrtle Beach. I found a large class ring and returned it. The owner said he had lost it in front of the Coral Beach. This is where I found the ring a year after it was lost.

In 2008 I found a hole in front of the Landmark. The few days that I detected this hole I found a large number of motel keys, all belonging to the Landmark. I have hunted north and south of this area and can not remember finding any Landmark keys. The keys were found where they were dropped.

Another piece of evidence that make gold ring travel unlikely at Myrtle Beach is the lack of pennies in the surf. Quarters and dimes far outnumber the pennies. On the upper beach pennies far outnumber the dimes and quarters. From my observations small children (penny losers) are a large portion of the upper beach crowd while adults make up the largest percentage of surf crowd (dime and quarter losers). It appears that the change pretty much stays where it is lost.

Another clue that things do not move around much at MB are 50 caliber shells and bullets that were placed on the upper beach during the two renourishment projects. In all of the years I have hunted the surf I have only found one 50 caliber shell in the surf (this was at Surfside Beach). The heavy bullets and shells do not move down the beach into the surf zone.

Why is there such a disparity on this subject of gold ring travel?

Myrtle Beach rarely has huge waves or hard running current. Recently, I visited the Outer Banks and witnessed twelve to fifteen feet waves pounding the beach. I was shocked. I have never seen such waves at MB. Also, at Ocracoke Island I saw fishermen casting monster sinkers into the waves and watched the current carry the rig down the beach at a rapid pace. Gold rings under these circumstances are probably going to move. It is my opinion that normally MB does not have the waves or current needed to move gold rings.

A major storm may move gold rings. The last major storm to hit Myrtle Beach was Ophelia in 2005. The gold rings have had six years to descend to the solid layer but very little opportunity to travel horizontally.

A few years ago Phil Alexander was asked to help find a pair of *very* expensive rings lost at Holden Beach.

"The rings were lost at the same time off a blanket that got caught with the rising tide. They were lost on an afternoon; I searched for them the next morning. The owner had the place marked where the blanket was and about fifteen minutes later the first ring was found. Both rings were very expensive antiques willed from her grandmother. The waves were running ninety degrees to the beach so I started a search pattern down the beach. After a couple of hours the owner said, "You might as well give up, it's gone forever." She went back to the cottage. But I was finding enough coins to keep detecting. At least a hundred yards down the beach I found the other ring. I'm glad she had described it to me or I would have thought it had nothing to do with the lost ring. Big diamonds with a black star sapphire; it was like looking at something from a pirates treasure.

The beach sand was hard and flat that day with a very strong wind pushing the waves straight down the beach. It rolled the ring further than I thought possible.

The overjoyed girl said the rings were never coming to the beach again."

In this scenario, with a very hard beach, the rings never had a chance to "descend." The ring that "traveled" also had a lot of surface area. I concede in this circumstance that ring movement is very possible.

A few months ago I found a spot in the surf that had a coquina rock bottom. Think of pumice. A scoop was worthless over this rock bottom. I had a day of small waves and excellent visibility (over one foot) and tried to drop down and fan. Wearing a twenty five pound weight belt the surge moved me around but I was able to retrieve five or six targets. At one point, I fanned and could see a small fist sized hole in the rock. I reached in with my fingers and pulled out a fishing sinker and a motel key. These two objects had moved around on top of the hard surface until they dropped into the small hole. I suspect gold rings on top of this hard surface will do the same. However, since the coquina is extremely holey I doubt that a gold ring moves very far before it finds a home.

• *Most* gold rings at *MB* reside very close to where they were lost.

• Small lightweight filigree rings with a large surface area have the best chance of traveling about.

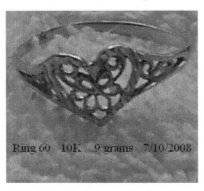

Ring 60 10K .9 grams 7/10/2008

One Cigarette

I was digging bobby pins with my new PI metal detector at Wrightsville Beach when one of the local metal detecting legends came down the beach and stopped to chat for exactly the length of one quick cigarette.

Sarge epitomized what a sergeant should be; tanned, muscular, rugged, bulletproof. In the course of one cigarette he let me know that there was far too much iron and junk on the beach to use a PI detector, that I needed to hit all the low spots, and that he could read the beach.

"I can take one look at the beach and tell whether or not it's worth swinging."

The late fall day was cool and I was surprised to see Sarge in cutoffs and barefoot; perhaps he was also impervious to cold. I watched him go, swinging the Excaliber, hitting a crease in the sand here and a wet spot there. There was something very "no-nonsense" about the man.

About forty-five minutes later he came by and showed me a gold ring he had gotten out of a "hole." In the time it took Sarge to find a gold ring I had filled my nail apron with bobby pins, nails, washers, bottle caps, and chunks of rusted metal.

Sand comes and goes, far more than people realize. A wise man once said that sand is a liquid. It is the movement, the ebb and flow, of the sand that makes metal detecting worthwhile or a complete bust.

As Sarge informed me, the treasure is in the low spots; the holes in the surf, the washouts, the horseshoes, the runnels, and the wet spots.

Always go low!!

The best beach for detecting has a water-filled hole or runnel with large shells and rocks in the bottom. This is a neon sign flashing the message, "Treasure Buried Here" complete with an arrow pointing at the hole.

Holes in the surf can be easy to spot or totally invisible. Even in the surf you are looking for the lowest point, the point closest to the treasure, the point closest to the shell layer, or hard pan.

• Reading the beach means that no matter where you are in the beach/surf environment you are always looking for the lowest point. Depressions are good.

How long do low spots stick around before they are filled in? I have seen a hole out in front of the Sea Crest Resort that lasted close to a week and I have also seen a wonderful hole in front of Ocean Annie's Beach Bar disappear overnight or in the length of one high tide. You can't wait and think the low spot or hole will be there the next low tide. That window of opportunity has a very nasty way of slamming shut. He who hesitates....

Get High!!

If you can, by all means get high...to take a look at the beach. A penthouse room with a view of miles of beach would be the ultimate. A good pair of binoculars or a telescope can help you spot the low spots. A Cessna would be nice. Even a look from a pier can give you a good view of a couple of miles of beach in each direction.

Sand Gauges; Rocks, Pilings, Groins, Sandbags, and Storm Drains

There are gauges I look at to judge how much sand is on the beach.

Before the sand renourishment project of 2008-09 there were large rocks showing in several locations at low tide. These included Hurl Park, 14th Ave. Pier, 2nd Ave Pier, and an area north of 82nd Ave. North.

As of April, 2011 none of these rock areas are visible due to the renourishment sand. It may take years for these rocks to show again.

The pilings on piers are another good gauge of sand depth or movement. Someone has nailed tar paper nails, the ones with the large round plastic disc, to the pilings at Apache pier. There is also a vertical box strapped to one of the pilings and it is a good indicator of sand depth.

The pilings on the 14th Ave Pier, below the restaurant, have concrete in rubber sleeves. These sleeves were

visible before the renourishment and have only just recently become visible again (April 2011).

Pawleys Island has groins, concrete and rock fingers
built perpendicular to the shore to trap sand. At times the
sand is eroded to the point that one can see under the edge
of the groin. Also, at times, the sand will be piled high on
one side of the groins and deeply cut on the other side.

At Ocean Isle there is a place where, on rare occasions of intense erosion, sandbags show up in the middle of
the beach. When these sandbags appear the detecting is
excellent.

Storm drains, concrete and plastic, are used at many
locations along the Grand Strand. At Christmas of 2010
none of the huge black plastic storm drains south of Apache
Campground were visible. Three months later, several of
the storm drains are showing and one was sticking out of
the sand at least fifteen feet, a clear sign of upper beach
erosion. I was at this location yesterday, May 10, 2011, and
the storm drains are buried again, sanded-in.

Many times upper beach erosion does not bode well
for lower beach/surf area metal detecting because the sand
has simply moved lower on the beach. Recently, winter of
2011, the upper beach eroded and left a shear wall drop-off

of three feet. I was out before the sun came up digging coins. I dug 175 coins that day...and no gold items. Seldom has the upper 1/3 of the beach been kind to me when it comes to gold finds. I have found a few gold items at the top of the beach but very few.

Sand is a Liquid

The largest single element that determines a detectorist success is sand.

Sand moves incredibly fast and slow. We are at the mercy of the wind, the waves, and the sand.

The other morning I was detecting a shell bed line about half way down the slope from the top of the beach. This was the only place that I was finding a few targets. The waves were at mid-tide and rising. A single wave shushed up above my path and receded. The shells were gone! A single wave carried enough sand with it to cover the shell bed. Most of the shells were small and their profile was probably only ½" to 1"above the sand. I've witnessed this sanding in process a number of times.

If the wave period is ten seconds we can extrapolate that a few inches of sand could be added in one minute and easily over a foot per hour.

I've also seen a strong NE wind shear three feet of sand off the top of the beach in one high tide cycle.

Most baffling of all is when a runnel or a hole appears in the middle of the beach without any major wind. It just shows up. These are mysteries of the beach, something akin to dark matter.

On the other end of the sand movement bell curve is when the beach sands-in and day after day of nice summer weather does nothing but bring more sand onto the beach. If summer lasted longer it would not be unreasonable to see a sandy beach all the way to Bermuda.

Hateful is Better

Nice weather with gentle breezes, generally, fills in the beach. Hateful weather with strong winds, 20 mph+, that run at an acute angle to the beach move massive amounts of sand and leave holes and depressions and cuts. Bring on the hateful weather, bring it on! Now, if only those sandbags will show up again.

Beach Erosion is King

Successful beach detectorists hunt for erosion. These are the areas that give up the gold rings.

Not all beaches are created equal. Some parts of the beach erode much more often than other parts of the beach. There are places along the Grand Strand that I avoid detecting simply because they never seem to erode. Likewise, the opposite is true; there are places that consistently erode and provide an opportunity to score.

Sunset Beach, NC rarely erodes. It is actually gaining sand. It has never been renourished. Phil Alexander lives in Shallotte, NC and has hunted Sunset Beach hundreds of times. A good day is ten coins. Some very nice jewelry has been found there but if I were to give it a scorecard it would get a three (out of ten).

Ocean Isle, NC often erodes. Houses on the north end have been sandbagged to keep them from washing away. OI has been renourished heavily and will probably always need renourishment. I do not hunt OI very often, because it is such a long drive from my place in MB, but have done well there. It would get a seven, maybe even an eight. I have found two of my best finds, a trophy ring and a pendant with a ¾ carat diamond, at OI.

There are places at MB that year after year the lifeguards put out the "no swimming" signs because of rip tides. How is it that holes in the sandbar exist in exactly the same spot every year? Why do some portions of the beach erode on a regular basis and other areas remain unscathed?

North Myrtle Beach was in desperate need of re-nourishment in 2007-8. The sand was gone all the way back to the dunes. Today (2011), NMB is eroding quicker than the rest of MB. It may be in part that it was renourished first and has had more time to erode. Another factor is that the renourishment program placed half as much sand at NMB as MB. (http://www.sac.usace.army.mil/?action=programs.myrtle _beach).

Regardless of the reasons, NMB is showing holes with rocks and shells while MB is badly sanded-in.

When I confronted Phil with this question of why some areas erode and others did not he said that it was due in part to the underwater topography or features beyond the low tide line. He also went on to say that before the hurricanes took out many of the piers along the Grand Strand that the areas near the piers were always good hunting because of holes gouged out by the waves.

Swashes, tributaries that enter the Atlantic, also affect the erosion nearby. Withers Swash is constantly changing course as it enters the Atlantic. I find it humorous that MB brings in heavy equipment to dig the swash a new channel straight out to sea. One day of tides and the new channel is filled in and once again the swash goes where it wants to go. The same is true of Singleton swash south of Apache Pier. Huge amounts of money have been spent to keep the swash from eroding the beach to the north and south.

The area north of Apache Pier has not been renourished because it lacks public access and yet this area has plenty of sand. I detected this area quite a bit when I first moved to MB but seldom did well.

Surfers frequent one area at NMB because the waves are better. The underwater shelf is conducive to building bigger waves.

Hunting the beach regularly will help find the better spots. Keep a notebook or journal of where you find the gold. Be open minded as you come out onto the beach...but also realize there was a reason that you found that gold ring where you did and its name is Erosion.

Not all beaches are created equal.

Clues and the Power of Observation

Workin' on Mysteries without any Clues   Bob Seger

The beach and surf are full of clues as to where a gold ring lies if you are observant.

Erosion Clues

Rocks and big shells are the number one clue to finding a low spot and the gold. This holds true for the beach and the surf, even in the summer. If I am in a hole in the surf and bumping my toes into fist sized rocks and conch shells I am digging lots of treasure. If I see a washout or runnel on the beach and I see fist sized rocks, or bricks, or chunks of concrete, or large shells I am highly confident that a gold ring is nearby.

The Foot Test for Gold. This past summer I was detecting the beach with my Sovereign and I kept looking at a fairly deep channel in the surf. It kept calling me. I would have to go back to the VW to get my Excaliber. I wanted some indication that it would be worth the walk. I took off the Sov and laid it on the beach. Then I walked into the surf and wandered around...until my feet bumped some big shells. Bingo! I sprinted back to the VW, got the Excaliber, and within half an hour I found a nice 14K mans ring.

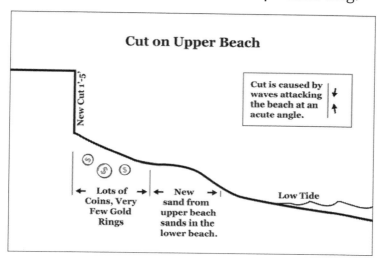

The second most obvious sign of erosion is an upper beach cut. It reminds me of the mesas out in Colorado. Waves traveling down the beach have sheared off a wall of sand. If you like digging coins until you drop, this is a bonanza for you. Last winter we had heavy South winds and were blessed with a 2'-3' upper beach cut. That day I found 175 coins and no jewelry. None, not even a belly button thingy or a toe ring.

It is my experience that there are very few gold rings below the cut. And for the most part, the gold rings are lightweight rings...mostly women's rings.

Another sign of erosion is a washout. The low tide line has a horseshoe shape in it. Sometimes there will be a series of washouts like the picture below.

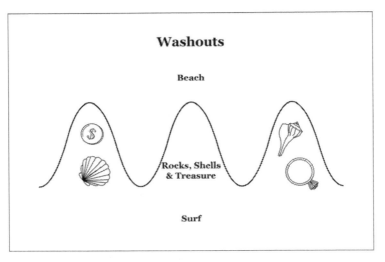

Washouts

Beach

Rocks, Shells
& Treasure

Surf

Not every washout has treasure. Some washouts, like the one in the picture below, are not deep enough to get you down to the shell/rock layer.

Other channels or washouts that look poor can actually hold the gold. In the picture below there were rocks in the channel just beyond the point where the person is looking for shells and I found a gold wedding band. Notice how the beach is slightly sunk down at that point. This rock area was no bigger than ten foot square.

Often times the beach will have a crease in it, defined by dark wet sand below the crease. I noticed long ago that detecting was better above the crease.

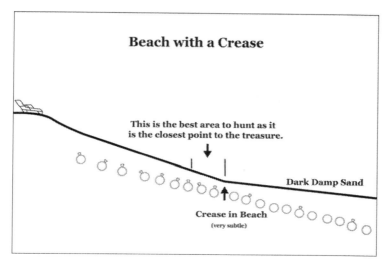

Beach with a Crease

This is the best area to hunt as it
is the closest point to the treasure.

Dark Damp Sand

Crease in Beach
(very subtle)

Steep banks and the area below steep banks are often excellent detecting along the Grand Strand.

Damp areas on the beach are a clue that the area is lower and has less sand over the treasure.

Clues to Bad Conditions

Just as there are plenty of clues to good conditions there are also clues to poor conditions. When you see bad conditions you change locations, run and gun.

The *flat beach* is a boring beach and shows no erosion whatsoever. It usually indicates that the beach is sanded-in. The incline is very shallow and if you look up and down the low tide line, it is straight. There are no shells showing. Sand and sand and more sand. The shallow incline will continue into the surf all the way to the sandbar. People wading in the surf will be thirty yards from shore and still be only knee deep. Boring and unproductive!

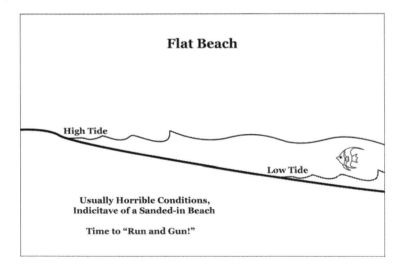

Flat Beach

High Tide

Low Tide

Usually Horrible Conditions,
Indicitave of a Sanded-in Beach

Time to "Run and Gun!"

The *horrible hump* is despicable. It will rise out of the beach, a giant mound of sand running parallel with the low tide line, covering up the lower beach and the treasure. Horrible humps can be formed from the top of the beach being eroded and the sand moving lower on the beach or the sand can come out of the surf area. This occurs when the waves are small and coming directly into the beach. The small waves gently push the sand up the beach. It is incredible how fast a horrible hump can appear. One day you can have an eroded lower beach and the next there will be five feet of new sand humped up. *Do not hunt the horrible hump!*

A trough will develop above the horrible hump at mid-beach that looks like a runnel. It is a fake runnel that collects pull tabs and bottle caps.

If the horrible hump has a redeeming quality it's that sometimes the area in the surf just below the HH has a trough that may be deep enough to hold gold rings.

Hard sand underfoot is a good sign. Mushy slop sand is newly deposited sand, sand that has sloughed off and covered up the lower beach. Worthless lightweight targets will be in the slop. Always concentrate your efforts on the hard sand areas.

Target Clues

Are you upset when you dig down a foot and find a pull tab or a bottle cap? You shouldn't be. You have just been given a clue to solving the puzzle. Pull tabs and bottle caps are lightweight hobos; riding the waves here and there. Most are found relatively shallow. A pull tab or bottle cap that is buried a foot deep is a very bad sign, a sure sign that the beach is badly sanded-in. Run away, run away.

I find very few pull tabs and bottle caps in the surf; the wave action keeps them beach bound.

It is my belief that many of the pull tabs and bottle caps come out of the storm drains that empty onto the beach.

Sunglasses are lightweight and because of their large surface area do not drop through the sand well; most are found shallow. If sunglasses are found deep it is because the beach is sanded-in; the sand has been deposited on top of the sunglasses. On rare occasions at Myrtle Beach when the surf water is clear you can see sunglasses skittering around on the ocean bottom.

Sinkers are also a good clue to where the gold lies...except near piers or at Holden Beach. Holden Beach was renourished from a channel that held millions of fishing sinkers.

In the surf, quarters, sinkers, and gold are often roommates.

50 caliber shells and bullets were found almost daily on the beach right after the renourishment. Now, three years later, I find them only when there has been some erosion. They are a very good sign if you find one *shallow* (less than 10"); slow down and work the area. If however you find a 50 caliber shell or casing very deep it can indicate that there is too much sand on the beach to find heavier items; gold rings.

Iron on the beach is another clue that one is near the base layer and the gold. There are two places at MB that drive me nuts with nulling and chopped off signals. I have avoided these areas due to the challenge that the iron presents. The gold rings are there but it takes patience and tenacity to extract them. A small coil is often used to isolate good targets amidst the iron.

Recently Ron Guinazzo (Chicago Ron on the Surf and Sand Forum) found a spot on a small beach at Lake Michigan that was eroded by large waves. In less than three weeks Ron found 34 gold items of which 27 were gold rings. The spot was also littered with iron making metal detecting close to impossible. Ron resorted to using a sifter and was rewarded with fifteen gold items; twelve gold rings, two gold chains, and one medallion. How much iron was there? On the day I spoke with Ron he had found two more gold rings with the sifter. He also stated that he found twenty pounds of rusted nails and other iron objects. Sifting is brutally hard work but as Ron has proven, it is deadly when iron is overwhelming.

If you decide to sift the beach please fill in your holes and remove all metal items, iron included, from the beach. Respect the beach. It is yours and mine and our children's and their children's.

Coin Clues

Dimes are wanderers. They travel about and act like they have no cents. Dimes tell us nothing for you can find a dime where there are no other signals. Dimes are clueless.

Pennies too are wanderers but to a lesser extent than dimes. The upper beach is usually filled with pennies from the kids. In the beach environment zinc pennies will be riddled with holes and chewed in half one year after being minted. Corroded zinc pennies will drop out of the high tones into the gold sounds, the mid-tones and sometimes even lower. Sandy blob pennies have lived for some time on the beach and usually show up during beach erosion.

Nickels and quarters have enough heft to them that they normally do not travel far, at least this holds true most of the time at Myrtle Beach. I find gobs of quarters in the surf in a good hole.

If however I am finding only deep quarters, say fifteen inches down, and few or no other coins, it tells me that there is too much sand in that area to be productive.

Green coins are beautiful; evidence that the coin has been buried for quite some time and that there has been some erosion. Finally enough sand has been taken out above the green coin that it is within range of my detector. A thick encrustation on a green coin is a clue to slow down and really critique the area.

Holes...A Week in the Surf

Holes in the surf are absolutely crucial to surf hunting success. Follow me into the surf for a week. The following posts were put on the Surf and Sand Forum at www.thetreasuredepot.com

Ring Daddy #49 and #50...OH MY!!!!!
Posted by Foiled Again Jim
Date: Sunday, June 29, 2008

8:20 I was in the water trying a spot that I have beat up for a couple of weeks. The targets were in deep water and the waves head slapped me for each signal. I decided to move into shallow water and there too, were just a few signals. After an hour and a half of this I looked down the beach and see a hole in a spot that I have never seen a hole. In five minutes I am in the new hole. OMG!!! Targets everywhere. 47 quarters. 91 coins and three tokens. $13.79 in change. 127 targets retrieved. This does not include the targets that I left because they were too deep. Here is the mess.

This is the 14K wedding band. 9.2 grams

This is my first platinum/18K gold ring for the year. 8.2 grams

Out of the water at 12:20. Four hours of digging insanity. I can't wait for tomorrow!!! Yeeehaw!!!!

Ring Daddy #51, 52, 53, 54
Posted by Foiled Again Jim
Date: Monday, June 30, 2008

Went back exactly where I was yesterday. The hole was still open and held a lot of targets. Broke my quarter record...52 quarters today. Also, broke my all time most change amount. $15.34. 100 coins exactly and three tokens. 133 total targets.

Tied my record for gold rings in one outing. Four. This one is 10K

These two came back to back. I had three in the first hour and a half. This one is 14K. Pretty ring.

This one is 10K

I knew there was at least one more out there. 14K and the diamonds are real. 6.9 grams

You know where I will be tomorrow.

Ring Daddy #55
Posted by Foiled Again Jim
Date: Tuesday, July 1, 2008

Headed back to plunder the same hole...but it was starting to fill in. The rocks were not nearly as numerous.

26 quarters today, exactly half of what I got yesterday. $8.16 total coins.

I did manage to dredge up one gold wedding band. 14K 3.1 grams.

Ring Daddy #56 and 57
Posted by Foiled Again Jim
Date: Wednesday, July 2, 2008

I'm going to be late for a meeting. I hunted too long. Here's the mess.

Here's the wedding band.

Here's the itty bitty ring.

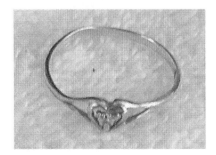

One man's trash is Jim's trash!!! Grrr…and Gold
    Posted by Foiled Again Jim
    Date: Thursday, July 3, 2008

Today was trash day. The hole I've been faithful to was pretty much filled in. So off I went down the beach, digging trash here and there.

After three hours and forty five minutes I was back to old faithful hole and this nice gold bracelet showed up. Why in the world do I have to wait till the very end to find something??? At least I got a little bit of gold. 10K   13.5 grams. The other necklace is silver.

Ring Daddy #58
Posted by Foiled Again Jim
Date: Saturday, July 5, 2008

Well yesterday was pretty dismal. One of the lowest target counts in a long time. Today I started in the hole that I've been beating up for a week. Finally, my girlfriend, Diana, came down and gave me some water. I jumped out of the hole and headed south. Found a new hole. Quite a few targets. This pic does not show the scuba mask that I snagged on the end of my coil (I couldn't see it till I walked out of the water) or the two giant pieces of chaise lounge chair or the 10' of electrical wire wrapped in electricians tape. Man I hate all the kids!!! I had one child bump into the wooden handle on my scoop while I was shaking it out.

This was one of the first targets in the new hole. 10K 5.0 grams.

You know where I will be tomorrow morning.

I was asked on the Surf and Sand metal detecting forum to elaborate about the "hole". This was my response.

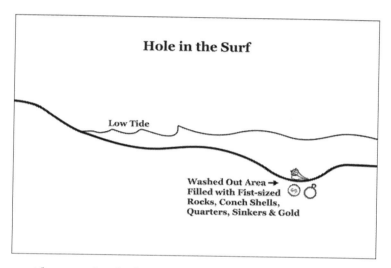

Ah yes, the hole. Holes in the surf are everything at MB. Without a hole I find almost nothing. Holes are caused by wave and water movement. I can read the water most of the time to see a hole. The waves break on the outer sandbar and then as the water comes across the sandbar one can see the smoothness. As the water leaves the sandbar it again wants to be a wave. If the waves are big, there is a hole at this point. If it seems that the waves are small or not much change from the sandbar there is no hole. Sometimes you can just see the dark blue of the hole. I always wear polarized sunglasses to help spot holes. Sometimes there is a channel with current in it that is parallel with the beach. This deepening often has lots of targets but depending on how much current there is and how deep it is, can be extremely hard to work. Here is the ultimate clue at MB.

You will feel the sand under your feet change to gravel, then to shells and then to big shells and rocks. When I find an area with big shells and rocks I will find treasure and usually a lot of it. If the low tide line is straight, it does not bode well. If the low tide line is up and down or has horse-shoes I usually do well. In the end...I need a hole. And I have to have shells in my scoop. Hope this helps.

Let's analyze the week of June 29th, 2008.

The two main characters were the holes of June 29th – July 3rd and July 5th.

The first hole was loaded with targets. Often times the targets were very close together and on occasion I would corral two coins in the same scoop. Quarters and dimes made up almost 60% of the targets. Everyday I found sinkers in this hole. A quick glance at the pictures confirmed what I already knew; there were few pull tabs or bottle caps. A hole normally has very little lightweight trash. This hole lasted four days, from Sunday through Wednesday. Thursday I gave up on the hole and only returned when I wasn't getting anything anywhere else. It gave up nine gold rings and the gold bracelet in five days.

The second hole I worked on Saturday and got another gold ring. It was a new beginning. I finished the week with ten gold rings and the gold bracelet. I owe it all to the depressions beneath the waves filled with large shells, rocks, and gold.

What Makes a Hole So Full of Treasure?

A hole is a depression, a washed out area that gets us closer to where the treasure stops its vertical descent through the sand. At Myrtle Beach there are four distinct places in the surf that the treasure comes to rest; the shell layer, the peat layer, coquina rock, or hardpan. This subject was touched on in the "Where are the Gold Rings?" chapter however I feel it is vitally important to emphasize the importance of finding these *solid* areas.

The shell layer is a solid layer of shells, making it difficult for lost treasure to drop further.

The peat layer is a hard layer usually found below the sand; however I have found areas stripped of sand and the peat layer was totally exposed. It feels spongy underfoot and is very hard to dig even with a stainless steel scoop. Imagine trying to dig carpet padding. I would think that nothing could go below this but I find coins and gold rings embedded in the first few of inches of this nasty stuff. Forcing the stainless steel scoop into this layer is tough and the peat comes out in black chunks. Once the scoop with the large chunks clears the water, then the nasty smelling chunks must be broken apart to find the target. Coins are black and extremely hard to see. This is much more work per target than working over a shell layer. I have yet to figure out a good way to deal with this mess.

Coquina rock is found at several places along the Grand Strand. Sometimes the coquina is buried beneath the sand. Whenever I get over coquina rock I have targets. This is an *extremely* challenging place to work. The coquina is wickedly sharp, jagged, cemented together micro-shells. It will cut you in a heartbeat. Then the sharks will come. The treasure nestles down in little holes in the solid rock. Some of the targets are embedded in the rock. A scoop is worthless. Dropping down and fanning the target is a poor solution in that the viz is extremely poor most of the time. Also, dropping down and fanning means being pushed around by the surge over the top of this razor rock. Coquina will eat up a coil. A coil swung over sand may last years, a coil banging into and being scraped across coquina may not last a month.

The hardpan is hard mud with a thin layer of soft mud on top. The trick here is to slice off a very thin layer of hardpan with the target. I found a hardpan/mud hole near Cherry Grove before the renourishment. This hole was a source of frustration. The best description I can think of is standing in chin deep surf on the edge of a cereal bowl loaded with treasure. When I would swing my detector into the hole I would get signals...but I could not retrieve them. I picked at targets around the edge knowing that the real treasure was oh so close but not obtainable.

This hole brings up another question/point. This hole was too deep for my normal water detector-scoop setup. It is indeed rare that a hole is this deep at MB. Why is that? Why are most holes in the surf less than chin deep? If anyone out there knows or has a theory, please send me an email.

What Causes a Hole to be Formed in the Surf?

I dunno. I do know that there have been numerous times when I've been in a hole and the waves were coming from two directions and crossing at the hole. It is like detecting in a washing machine.

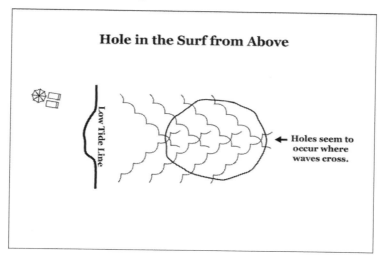

Hole in the Surf from Above

Low Tide Line

← Holes seem to occur where waves cross.

Are All Holes in the Surf Filled with Treasure?

Absolutely not. A true treasure hole gets the metal detectorist close to the shell/peat/coquina/hardpan layer. There are many low spots out in the surf that are just not deep enough to reach the gold.

How Big are Holes in the Surf?

Holes can be the size of your living room or the length of a motel. A few years ago I spotted a small, per-fectly round hole in the surf about 20'-30' across. This was a very unique hole for it had very steep sides, almost as if someone had used a cookie cutter and cut a hole into the sand. I stepped down into the hole twelve to sixteen inches and immediately got a signal; a pair of sunglasses. I worked  around the edge and then gridded back and forth. In the end I got a total of eight signals, two being gold wedding bands. Even the wedding bands were a bit strange in that both were almost exactly the same size, about six grams. One was yellow gold and one was white gold.

I also had the pleasure of plundering an extremely large hole in front of the Sea Crest Resort. In the beginning this hole was the same length as the Sea Crest motel. This hole lasted almost a week and I found a number of gold rings and a very nice gold sailor's pendant.

As the week wore on this hole filled in on the north side and lengthened on the south side...it was morphing down the beach. At last, the south end turned to the sea and then the hole filled in.

Is there a method for plundering a hole?

I try to hunt the deepest water first for the obvious reason; the rising tide will soon make the deepest area inaccessible. I work slow and grid. I try to use palm trees, motel rooms to mark my progress. If I have to leave a hole before I am finished I always try to line up a couple of objects so I can return to where I left off.

Hole vs. No Hole

Holes in the surf are everything to a surf detectorist. If I have a choice between a hole in the surf in front of Greg's Motel with six rooms and a flat sandy bottom in front of the Ritz Carlton, the hole in the surf in front of Greg's Motel would get my nod.

Are There "Super Holes", Places in the Surf Where Heavy Items Collect?

I personally have never found what I would call a super hole.

I've asked quite a few people who detect the surf this question and only two gave me a resounding, "Yes!" One said that he was diving in the Caribbean off of a beach and ran into a ledge where the gold collected. The other was also diving a hole that he had spotted from a small plane. He said it was full of sinkers and sinkers and more sinkers and gold.

My experience at MB is that the treasure seems fairly evenly distributed. If I find a hole with large shells and rocks I will find a lot of quarters, a few sinkers, odds and ends, and some gold.

It is not farfetched to think that the surf would sort items by weight and size, especially if the area was hit by large storms.

Perhaps someday, I will stumble upon that magical place; a hole that glistens with gold rings, chains with diamond studded crosses, bracelets, Rolex watches, a carpet of sparkling, shimmering sunshine beneath the waves.

The Golden Runnel of 2007

Somewhere near the end of March 2007, I walked out on the beach and there it was; a trough (runnel) in the middle of the beach that ran for three miles, from Ocean Annie's Beach Bar to the Myrtle Beach Travel Park.

Looks are often deceiving when it comes to beach runnels and with good reason. What made the runnel? Was it even a real runnel or a fake runnel? Fake runnels are made by the beach sanding in and leaving a crease that looks very much like a true runnel. A real runnel is one gouged out by the waves and is often filled with large rocks and shells. Real runnels contain treasure. Fake runnels contain pull tabs and bottle caps; lightweight junk.

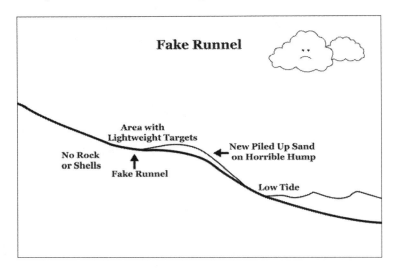

The trough at low tide had knee deep water and as I waded I began to pick up some coins. More important than the coins was the presence of large shells and fist sized rocks.

Here it was, the "trough" of which I had only heard rumors.

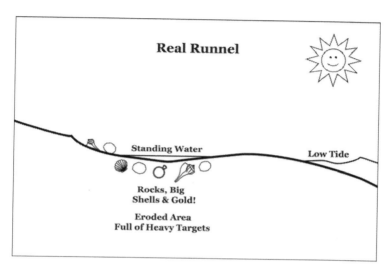

Phil Alexander related a story of a trough that he had found at North Myrtle Beach. He described the trough as a "clear mountain trout stream." He said you didn't need a detector. Gold rings were visible in the crystal clear water. A man came down the beach and showed Phil a beautiful gold chain that he had just picked up out of the trough.

Day after day I waded into the runnel and usually was rewarded with at least one gold ring, sometimes two.

Then the second worst thing that can happen happened (remember the first worst thing is to find a gold ring on the beach). I got a phone call from an architect to do some store surveys in Florida. It would only be a week and pay very well. I waffled but in the end I took the temporary job.

Of course, the week of work seemed like an eternity as my mind was doing constant flashbacks of gold rings in the scoop.

At last, I arrived back in MB and sprinted out onto the beach.

Remnants of the trough, pockets of water, a low spot here, a low spot there, were still visible. The beach was almost through filling in the trough. I found one more gold ring before the trough was no more.

How many gold rings had the "job" cost me? I will never know.

In Economics they call it Opportunity Cost. What was the true cost? The choice I made ended up costing me gold rings and the pleasure of enjoying my life on the beach.

The money I received is long gone and so is that week.

For a short time the beach opened up, a rare event, and I gave away my opportunity for money. I hang my head in disgust when I think about that decision. How could I have been so blind?

Sometimes, when the wind is just right and the sea smell reaches my nostrils, I close my eyes and see the silver flecked water in the gold filled runnel that ran for miles.

Someday the golden runnel will return.

Run and Gun

This may be the most important chapter in this book.

All beaches are not created equal. Some lose sand and some gain sand. Over the years Myrtle Beach will continue to erode and Sunset Beach will continue to gain sand. In the short term, day to day, all beaches erode and gain sand due to wind and wave action.

Also, as pointed out in the Better Gold chapter some sections of beach have better jewelry to find.

I hate it!! Dadgum, I hate it. I loathe it. What I am going to tell you runs counter to what I believe in. Personally, I hate cars and the pollution they cause. I wore out the pavement walking and riding my bike to the beach from the KOA campground. This "green" approach is highly ineffective for finding gold.

To be a truly successful beach/surf hunter you must move around or else wait for erosion or a hole to show up at your local beach. You might wait a long, long time.

You can not wait for erosion to come to you; you have to chase it down.

A few winters ago, Vince and I detected the local beach and were coming up with nada, zip, and also some zilch. We needed something to break the silence in the headphones. One morning we jumped in the VW and took a trip to Pawleys Island, a forty-five minute drive from the campground. The upper third of the beach was eroded back to the dunes. We dug coins and coins and coins for the next week, close to 1500 coins. We dug until we were too tired to dig. We also dug a few gold rings. Man was that fun!

Run and Gun is parking as close to the beach as possible, jumping out and running out to the beach to take a look, determining if it looks swing-worthy. The jumping out and running is so you don't have to pay parking. Nothing? Jump back in and go down the beach a couple of miles and check again. Run and gun until you see something interesting; a hole, a cut, black sand, a trough. Sometimes the whole world seems sanded-in but often, just a few miles away, there is a hole carpeted with coins and gold.

The reason that Run and Gun is so effective is that all beaches face different directions and they erode differently. If you stand at the end of Apache Pier (the longest wooden pier on the east coast), you will note the C curvature of the beach and motels going to the northeast and south.

The beach at Pawleys Island faces ESE (a bit south of directly E). Myrtle Beach at the 14th Ave. Pier faces directly SE. North Myrtle Beach faces SExS. Holden Beach faces SSE (almost directly S). It is easy to see why some locations are eroded and others are sanded-in. The wind and waves attack each beach differently.

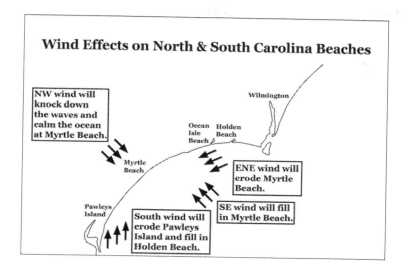

I want to scratch where it itches. I want to hunt where there is erosion.

Can a sanded-in area help with your next stop?

Last winter Vince and I hit the Windy Hill area and saw that it was sanded-in. We went north, checking every couple of miles. I was getting the distinct impression that the further north we went, the worse the conditions were getting.

"Vince, let's go the other way."

We hopped on Hwy 31 and sped south, getting off at Surfside Beach. Long story short, we found some erosion and had a good day detecting.

• To be a truly successful beach/surf hunter you must move around or else wait for erosion or a hole to show up at your local beach. Use Run and Gun to find the erosion and the gold.

Workable Conditions

A dad with two kids entered the surf and I watched the current take them to the north. Within a few minutes they were a quarter of a mile from their entry point. As I waded in to knee depth I felt the pull of the current. As I got chest deep I leaned back and dug my feet into the hard sand to stay put. A smooth, graceful mid-tone signal came into the headphones. Oh my, that's a gold ring if I ever heard one. I brought the scoop around and using all my strength tried to place it in front of my left foot. The current ripped the scoop forward, a stainless steel kite. I fought back. The tireless current was stronger than my mightiest attempt to place the scoop. The battle raged. I would come so close to positioning the scoop only to have it wing away. Fifteen minutes of futile attempts. Just as I was saying, "To hell with it," the tip of the scoop found its spot. I raised my foot to push on the scoop and was blown downstream twenty feet. The current had won.

But my resolve kicked in. Resolve sounds better than beat up ego. I trudged back upstream and found the target. I then turned to the shore, located some landmarks, and counted my steps as I left the surf. I walked to the car and put on my thirty pound weight belt. I returned to the golden target and began the fight once more to set the scoop. Insidiously the tide began to rise. Was there another way? Perhaps I should run over to Wal-Mart and pick up a boat anchor, place the anchor upstream, repel down to the target, and fan the bottom. After forty-five minutes I gave up.

Fast moving currents that will not let you set your scoop are not workable conditions.

Surf hunting is a contact sport. Large angry waves that suck you off the bottom of the ocean, then spin you catawampus, then drag you across the bottom while your stainless steel scoop gyrates wildly trying desperately to chop holes in your body will soon make you into a beach hunter. You only need to experience this once to understand the concept of workable conditions. Fearing for your life is not workable conditions.

I personally have never been in a rip tide. Gene Patrick, another metal detectorist in the KOA campground, was flushed out to sea while swimming. The TV commercials tell you to remain calm and swim parallel to shore until you are clear of the rip tide. Gene says this is horsehockey. His account is that panic instantly grips you as you are propelled away from shore and you will struggle violently to gain some control. Fatigue comes very quickly and then deep panic really sets in. Gene was extremely lucky to make it back to shore. The ingredients for a good nightmare would be to be caught in a rip current with my detector and scoop and weight belt. Oh my!

Everyone has a different tolerance for pain or discomfort. An occasional small wave that breaks over ones head, to me, is tolerable. Actually being head slapped by a wave is worse than having it break over your head. Having your headphones knocked off your head every couple of minutes is not workable conditions.

Conditions change with the tide. A hole may not be workable two hours before low tide but as the tide drops the sandbar may be absorbing more of the wave and the waves may become small enough to be workable. If you know a hole is out there, work the beach until you have your opportunity to be productive. And it may not be today or tomorrow. And maybe the hole will fill in before the opportunity presents itself. However, when conditions are workable seize the opportunity by the throat, stare hard into its steely eyes, and bring home the gold.

Please, No Deeper

I got a wisp of a signal. Just under the 1/2" layer of sand was a layer of big shells. I probed with the tip of my shovel just to find a spot to penetrate one inch. Then I dug/scraped the sand and shells. Then another inch. Then another inch. I set the detector off to the side so I could use both hands on the shovel to dig. The hole was filling with water. I slashed at the hole. I kept digging and digging and digging. Then I'd pick up the detector and check. The target was still in the ever widening hole. I stood back and cussed, then dug some more. Then I picked up the detector and rechecked. Still in the hole. More cussing. Then it became a matter of principle. No, that's not it. It's a matter of ego. I would win! I would get whatever out of that hole. It was me against the shells and sand. I would win, no matter how deep I had to go. If I had to dig a three foot deep hole, six foot across, so be it. I dug more and more slop out of the hole. At last, a 50 caliber shell came out of the hole. I'd spent a huge amount of effort and time for one friggin piece of #@%* 50 caliber shell. I had also used up all of the ammunition in my cussing vocabulary. Now, I had to fill in the hole; more time and effort. Yeah, I want more depth so I can spend an hour digging one friggin hole to find a can bottom or a pull tab or a bottle cap.

OK, I'm going to say it. *I don't want more depth.* I am probably the only one out there that has the intestinal fortitude to say it.

I want less sand. I don't want to dig 20" for a very small possibility of a gold ring. I've done it. I don't like it. I want more targets at a humane depth and that means finding some erosion or a hole in the surf. The solution to finding more gold is less sand. You don't need a super deep detector to find gold if you find a hole in the surf. You don't need a deep detector to find gold if you have some erosion, a cut, a trough or runnel.

- Less Sand + Good Beach/Surf Detector= More Gold.

Seasons...The Winds of Change

The answer my friend is blowing in the wind, the answer is blowing in the wind. Bob Dylan

Winter Winds

Winter is the time to be rescued by the Myrtle Beach Police or Fire Department. Twice I have been waved to shore by uniformed officers. They find it strange to see a man clad in a wetsuit detecting the surf in fifty degree water. Surfers are not given a second glance but a metal detectorist, deep in the surf, requires rescuing. He's an escapee or has not taken his medications and we need to save him.

Winter often gives you fifty percent of the puzzle, wonderful workable conditions. Cold northwest winds calm the ocean, so much so that the Atlantic takes on the appearance of a giant pond, with nary a ripple. Myrtle Beach faces southeast and the northwest winds knock down the incoming waves. A few hours of northwest wind and the Atlantic becomes a sheet of glass, a slumbering giant with one inch waves.

Wading around in the winter ocean when my movements are the only thing that is generating water movement is eerie. I am the only disturbance for miles. There are no crashing waves, no traffic noise from Ocean Blvd., no screaming kids, and only a few solitary folks out for a beach walk or hunting shark's teeth and the quiet is too quiet.

When I get a target and scoop the ocean bottom I think about the noise the scoop is making, the crunching in the sand. When I shake the scoop and the sand and small shells rattle around and fall through the holes and send out underwater vibrations, I wonder who is listening. I am all alone and so very small. There is a struggling movement under my foot as a skate or flounder escapes. My heart races.

Southerly winds bring erosion...if it is more SSW. SSW winds for Myrtle Beach are reverse nor'easters and do a nice job of stripping the beach of sand. SSW winds come off the fifty degree ocean and are brutally cold.

WSW winds blow sand off the top of the beach and fill the eyes and hair with grit. If you are on Weight Watchers you need to add points for the amount of sand eaten.

Nor'easters rarely come to Myrtle Beach, at least that is my experience for the last five years. In following the metal detecting forums for many years it is clear that the northeast coast gets nor'easters fairly often. This is a time when those detectorists north of Wilmington, NC take wheelbarrows out to the beaches and fill them with old silver and old gold class rings.

Before the renourishment project of 2008 it was common to find holes in the surf in the winter and I did well. Since the renourishment I have never found a decent hole in the surf; there's just too much sand. The whole complexion of detecting has changed. However, winter beach hunting can be very productive. In 2011 Vince and I found 39 gold/platinum rings from Jan. 1st through March 31st. On February 14th I found my second best ring find; a platinum with diamonds ring.

Birds; seagulls, terns, plovers, ducks and geese fill the winter sky or walk the deserted beaches. Seagulls stomp holes in the sand. Pigeons often gather against the upper beach drop-off to take in the warmth of the low hanging sun. For a few days each winter eagles migrate through the KOA campground and use the same branch on the same tree to watch for fish in the canal. One very cold morning an egret walked upon the clear sheet of ice and eyed the fish below.

Sea foam is a part of the winter beach. It will stick to your boots and coil and make you appear to be wearing those white furry boots that women wear in the ski lodges while swinging a white birthday cake.

Myrtle Beach rarely sees snow. A couple dustings of white per year are normal.

I've witnessed forty-four below zero in Gunnison, Colorado and had the snot in my nose freeze within three steps out the door. It was a dry cold without wind. Cold in Myrtle Beach is colder. A damp wind off the ocean can make sixty degrees a parka day. Metal detecting in a blowing winter rain on the beach, when your jeans become coated with a layer of ice, will soon have you looking at new golf clubs at Martins. I wish I had a nickel for every Canadian that comes to Myrtle Beach in the winter and says, "I could have been this cold and miserable back in Calgary."

Spring Winds

Spring is a time of crocuses, daffodils, blooming forsythia, and fickle flip-flop winds. Really, there is no spring in the Southeast. I have lived in the southeast long enough to know that spring last about two or three days. It is a hateful time of year; days upon days of 50's and 60's and cruel, blustery twenty mph winds. One never, ever knows what to wear. You pray for a seventy degree day and it never comes. Punxsutawney Phil predicts an early spring and after the sharp knife like winds cut through you day after day you wish there was a groundhog hunting season. Somewhere close to the 1st of May the winds quit and it is eighty degrees with no wind. Grrr! When the spring winds subside the beach/surf will start its summer pattern of sanding in.

The Weather Channel has a graph that shows a nice smooth curve with escalating temperatures. There is no way!! What the meteorologists have done is extrapolated Spring. They know that winter is cold and summer is hot and they just filled in the graph to make it look nice.

You can wear out a kite in the spring months in Myrtle Beach. Seesaw winds alternate from the south and north. At times, these winds will bring some excellent detecting. In the spring of 2011, there was substantial upper beach erosion followed by massive sanding in. There were also times when mid-beach to lower-beach washouts appeared with large shells and rocks in the bottom.

The ocean water temperature at Myrtle Beach hits seventy degrees about mid-May and the beach comes alive with frolickers in the surf.

The bikers are back in 2011 and if you are planning a vacation you might want to consider coming to or avoiding this event. Bikers lose very little jewelry; most never come out to the beach.

I hate you, Punxsutawney Phil, you lying rodent. I hate you and your shadow.

Summer Winds

One of the All Star Wrestlers brags, "I have crippled more men than polio!" This is also the boast of the summer beach.

"Water....water....wa... " I struggle up the last steps to the restaurant. Death is chasing me up the steps. The waitress brings me water and I down the glass and ask for more. I feel absolutely horrible. Sunstroke; too much sun and not enough water. Summer is dangerous.

I have sun burnt my feet so they swelled up and looked like red shoe boxes. I have sun burnt my eyes wading in the surf from the suns reflection on the water (they feel like someone threw gravel in them). I've rubbed blisters on my toes from wearing sandals. "Rubbed" is inaccurate. Do you remember what a wood rasp looks like? Here is the recipe for "rasping" blisters. Wear sandals that you do not normally wear. Wade into the water and get sand and small bits of broken shell under the straps. Wade out of the surf and walk ten feet. This causes the rasping. You are now the proud owner of four new blisters which will make your life a living hell for the next few days. Blisters show character.

A real man wouldn't detect without blisters. Of course you will walk all crippled up and this will work muscles that you don't normally use so they, the muscles, will cry out in pain but you tell those muscles to shut up so you can hear the painful screams from the blisters. Pain should be prioritized and since you have taken off your sandals to stop the rasping, the bottoms of your feet are now being burned by the sand as you hobble across the giant frying pan back to the car.

"Mommy, look at that poor crippled up man, jumping from one foot to the other, carrying his sandals and trying to swing his detector.....Should I tell him most people wear their sandals on their feet and that he should try to keep his swing level?"

"That would be nice dear." Mom is catching some rays and reading about the bat boy or the twenty three pound grasshopper.

The renourishment project enlarged the soft sand frying pan area at the top of the beach to the width of a football field. It is no longer possible to cross this area without sandals or shoes. The beach is a trap. The tourists cross the frying pan at 10:00 in the morning before the sand has warmed up. Then they try to leave the beach at 2:00 in the afternoon after the sand has reached maximum feet-frying temperature. Some tourists get a third of the way across the soft sand, their faces contorted with hideousness, turn around, and sprint back to the lower beach. Sprinting in soft sand carrying two kids, the cooler, the beach toys, chaise lounge chairs, and the beach tent is a slow sprint. I suspect that some of these barefoot people steal other people's sandals.

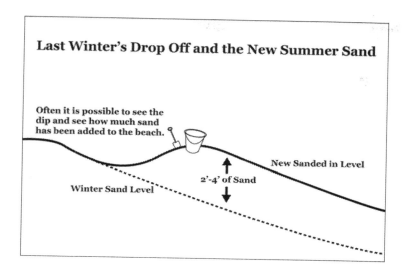

Last Winter's Drop Off and the New Summer Sand

Often it is possible to see the dip and see how much sand has been added to the beach.

New Sanded in Level

2'-4' of Sand

Winter Sand Level

"Oh, I'll bet you find all kinds of good stuff in the summer."

The immaculate assumption is that beach detecting in the summer is great. Wrongo!! This has to be the biggest misconception of summer beach hunting.

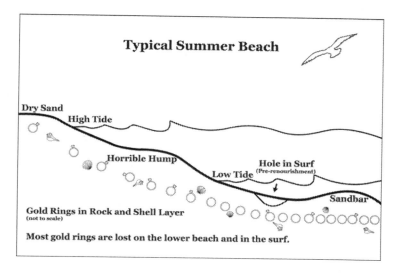

Typical Summer Beach

Dry Sand

High Tide

Horrible Hump

Hole in Surf (Pre-renourishment)

Low Tide

Sandbar

Gold Rings in Rock and Shell Layer (not to scale)

Most gold rings are lost on the lower beach and in the surf.

My twenty-eight cents day on the Fourth of July convinced me that summer can be a time when you swing until your arm falls off and find very little. Bionic arms are a good investment. It is logical to think that summer would be good for detecting because of the crowds. But the logic is lacking the knowledge of sand. If you want to stop the beach hunting machine from running, throw copious amounts of sand into the cogs and sprockets.

Memorial Day is the unofficial start to summer in Myrtle Beach.

Summer is a time of opposites; small winds and hurricanes. Daily small winds bring in sand to the beach, building mountains of sand on top of the new drops.

And yet off the African coast or in the Gulf of Mexico the waters are a hot breeding ground for hurricanes and tropical storms. Often times these storms bring torrential rains to the southeast. Hurricane Floyd brought fifteen inches of rain to North Carolina and overflowed the hog farm waste holding ponds. The spillage spewed into the ocean and turned the Myrtle Beach ocean water a poopy brown. When you're wading in the surf for treasure you notice things like this.

Tropical Storm Hanna brought incredible amounts of sand onto the beach. The plywood storage containers the lifeguards use were half buried in sand. Sea oats on the dunes that were five feet tall were suddenly eighteen inches high.

Hurricane Ophelia was a detectorist dream hurricane; slowly plodding along, making a loop, and then continuing north. The beach was stripped of sand down to the hardpan. A detector was optional equipment as there were many exposed coins lying on the beach.

Statistically, Myrtle Beach is overdue for a storm. http://www.hurricanecity.com/city/myrtlebeach.htm

The first week in September is the height of the hurricane season. It is also the week of the butterflies, a sky of yellow wings. I am unsure if these are butterflies that migrate through or simply hatch out by the thousands at this time.

Summer is night hunting; cheating the heat, seeing naked people in the surf, and finding a few new drops. I loathe the afternoon beach. Give me the evening, night, and early morning when the sea is at rest.

Summer pattern waves that travel more directly into the beach create sandbars. The intensity and the quickness of the waves determine whether the sand is deposited on the beach or away from shore in a sandbar. Quick, strong waves keep the sand in motion, not allowing it to settle on the ocean floor until it moves away from the beach, creating the sandbar. Smallish waves will let the sand settle on the beach.

Sandbars can benefit the surf hunter by breaking down incoming waves. The sandbar may also be built out of the sand that was residing in the surf zone or on the beach. Either way the sand has moved. It is up to the beach/surf hunter to find the depression filled with rocks and shells and gold.

Let's sum up summertime. It is too hot, dangerous, too many people and kids and sanded-in. The traffic is horrendous. Summertime is finding twenty eight cents in four hours in a blast furnace. It is also a time of mental cruelty from storms that bring more sand into the beach and surf area. It is my least favorite season.

Fall Winds

Fall is the lover you never want to leave. All of the seventy degree days that never showed up at the altar in the spring now stand in line to kiss the bride. One mellow day flows into the next. Her smooth caress, the unhurried maturity, the sweet wisdom and warmth are the traits of fall. Fall is living forever, afternoon naps and thinking about our place in all of it. It's time to linger and etch a memory of waves thundering through the pilings or pelicans riding the thermals above the motels. The night is full of stars and the first chill, the first winds from the north, and a harvest moon.

One can never predict the winds of autumn. It may be a left over hurricane or tropical storm, the mingling of the soft summer breezes with the more vibrant southern winds, or a taste of the coolness from the north. Fall is a time of transition; hybrid winds.

The beach sand is full of gold from the summer crowds, buried beneath the mountains of summer sand. A couple of days of heavy SSW wind or a baby nor'easter will have you doing the ring dance.

Some nights in my camper in the KOA campground I can hear the waves pounding the beach. I close my eyes and listen intently to the rhythm of the thunder, the six second pause and the low muffled hammer blow. I see the endless army of swells, rolling silver in the dark, tripping, falling, crashing. Tomorrow may be the day.

Chasing the Elusive Extra Low Tide

Early in my beach education I read about the importance of hunting during the extra low tide periods. Two times each month, during full moon and new moon, we are blessed with a few days of extra high and extra low tides...or at least that is what the tide charts tell us. *In theory*, more of the lower beach is exposed and you have more opportunities to find the gold.

I usually consult the tide tables at www.saltwatertides.com.

Sometimes the tide chart will tell us that the extra low tide will be as much as a foot or more below the norm. Today, as I write this, there is a new moon. The tide chart shows that Myrtle Beach will experience a -.3 low tide. This is not a significant extra low tide. However, it beats the +1.1 neap tide (the half moon phase) of March 19th, one week earlier, by almost a foot and a half. This can make a difference on how much lower beach is exposed...at least in theory.

I became obsessed with this extra low tide thing. I also noticed that extra low tides occurred close to or after midday or after midnight for Myrtle Beach. This has held true for the last several years. I can't ever recall extra low tides being in the early morning or late evening.

Years ago (before I moved to Myrtle Beach), I would drive two hundred miles in the pre-dawn hours from my home in Troutman, NC to Myrtle Beach, eager to experience the euphoria of the extra low tide. If I arrived early in the morning I would smile at the calm summer ocean. The flag out at the end of Apache pier would hang limp. At nine o'clock the flag would show some movement. By eleven o'clock the flag would stand out, stretched taut by the wind coming from the ocean. The waves slammed and pushed up the beach effectively covering the lower beach.

Time and time again this scenario played out. I was frustrated that I was never able to cash in on the extra low tide advantage. Was the extra low tide only a myth?

My observations led me to conclude that the daytime extra low tide was a myth.

I began to hunt the nighttime extra low tides at Myrtle Beach. During a full moon it can be a world of intense shadows and being able to see almost as clearly as during the day. During new moon it will be dark, very dark, the only light coming from the stars and the motels. This is a time when I am alert, aware of where I am and conscious of the night people wandering the beach.

Regardless of whether it is new moon or full moon, you will need a dependable light. I prefer the lights that clip onto a baseball cap.

On one of my early attempts at night hunting, six or seven years ago, the extra low tide at full moon paid off. I felt the breeze coming from the land, the ocean was alive with tiny flecks of silver and the waves gently shussed up the beach. At Apache Pier the beach ran further out than I had ever seen it. I swung the Sovereign and traveled out there, out where I had never been. I got a solitary signal...a strange sounding signal. I dug a quarter. The signal had not sounded like a quarter and I swung across the hole again. Another signal, a mid-tone came into the headphones. I dug and suddenly there was a gold ring lying in the moonlight, a heavy gold wedding band.

I swung down the quiet beach, watching four tiny sandpipers play tag with the small waves, amazed at the whirring quickness of their legs. Out in front of Ocean Annies, a local bar, I got another low signal at the low tide line; just barely a signal. I dug one shovelful of sand out and caught a glint of gold. I fell to my knees, reached down into the wet sand and felt the links of a chain. I pulled steadily, slowly the sand yielded and the chain was set free. I turned away from the motel and let the moon glisten the gold chain.

The night did not yield many targets, less than ten, but the two gold items made up for the lack of targets. The 14K chain was the heaviest gold chain I've ever found, 64 grams.

Had I found the elusive extra low tide?

After many years of hunting the extra low tide periods I've come to some conclusions.

The numbers in the tide charts are based on gravitational forces on the oceans. The numbers do not take into account storms or winds or wave movement.

The extra low tide during the day is largely a myth, a fable, a wisp of smoke. The extra low tide at night is real, very real, a friend of the beach hunter.

Why would this be so?

I ran upon the answer, a verification of what I felt I knew, in a book titled **Tideland Treasure** by Todd Ballantine. Todd explains how in the morning, the sun warms the land faster than the ocean. This creates an updraft over the land which pulls the cooler air over the ocean towards the beach. As the sun climbs in the sky this accelerates, the breeze from the ocean gains in strength and the waves build. Thus, you will almost always lose the extra low tide area of the beach to the building daytime waves.

Now, at night the cycle is reversed. The land loses the heat much quicker than the ocean and the warmth from the ocean rises, pulling the cool air from the beach toward the ocean. This air current knocks down the incoming waves or at least diminishes the wave's strength. This phenomenon coupled with the extra low tides often gives the nighttime hunter some extra beach to hunt.

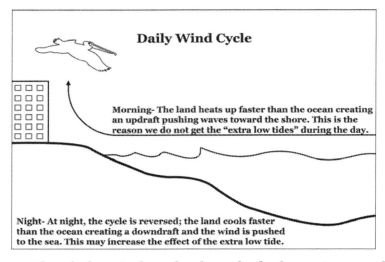

Daily Wind Cycle

Morning- The land heats up faster than the ocean creating an updraft pushing waves toward the shore. This is the reason we do not get the "extra low tides" during the day.

Night- At night, the cycle is reversed; the land cools faster than the ocean creating a downdraft and the wind is pushed to the sea. This may increase the effect of the extra low tide.

The daily wind cycle described above is one that probably takes place at your beach.

You can get the daily and ten day forecast for your locale at www.weather.com. This will give you some idea of the winds and how it will affect the wave height and strength at the beach. Another great source is the www.wunderground.com marine forecast for your area.

Be aware that the macro weather conditions, such as a front with strong winds, will sometimes nullify the extra low tide and daily wind cycle advantage.

Personal observations and a little science have helped me understand the elusive extra low tide.

• The extra low tides exist at night and rarely during the day.

Night Hunt

On the beach, where the waves have left a sheen, the moon is in the mirror at my feet. The same moon is overhead. It's a two moon night, one above and one below and I am in the world between.

A large brown crane has decided it is OK to share the surf with me as long as I keep my distance. I'm glad to have a companion, even if the friend is tall, thin and gangly, for the night is lonely. Motel lights weep into the night throwing indistinct shadows. The air is warm and heavy and there is no breeze.

A raft of diving ducks sits in the water at the far edge of my vision. How would it feel to be floating on the water, backlit by the moon while hungry eyes below searched for sustenance? Were there twenty ducks at dusk and nineteen at dawn? Did the sea wolves ever attack the eyeball moon lying on the water?

The coil on my metal detector flows back and forth, an inch above the beach, firing radio waves into the sand. A tiny hum is in the headphones, sounding like a far off beehive at the end of the orchard, the detectors threshold sound. When the radio waves bounce into something metal it severs the threshold with quiet meaning I have iron or a very deep target or an audible sound alerting me to a nonferrous piece of metal. Tonight the beach has too much sand and the only metal to be found are pull tabs off of beer and soda cans. The heavier objects are buried too deeply.

What about the surf?

At the far edge of the black Atlantic I cannot tell where the sea meets the sky for the moon and stars are also in the water. There are tens of muted stars, not thousands or millions of stars for the lights of the city of Myrtle Beach muddy the night sky. The moon is rippled by nervous little waves. The crane scans the sea, standing still, a statue. A million years ago it would have looked the same.

I wade knee deep into the surf and the stars, swinging the coil.

The tourists have left, the late September night beach is a place of semi-quiet. A trash truck beeps as it backs up at one of the motels and a lone crotch rocket shifts gears, whining angrily on Highway 17.

What is below the water's surface, unseen?

A small fish bumps my shin and I smile. Big fish eat smaller fish.

The surface of the water to my left begins to tremble. A few bait fish fly into the air trying to escape the carnage; the jaws with needle-teeth snap wildly at the school. More small fish flee the water and become airborne. Blues. The bluefish have the small fish surrounded and are dining. The darkness is alive with an acre of jumping baitfish, thousands of silver moonlit splashes.

Do the small fish know that their brethren are being eaten? Do they smell the blood and jump, or is it that they are always fleeing and the school has neared the surface and they just happen to break the water? Do the small fish know fear? Do they know about death? They have fish brains, how could they know?

I wade the shallows away from the excitement. The tide is moving out and further down the beach I can make out a scooped out area, a U in the low tide line. As I approach I begin to drop into the hole; knee deep, thigh deep, privates deep, naval deep. The moon has followed me and now I break the image with my metal detector shaft's movement.

Sound comes into the headphones. Quarter. My ears analyze the high tone of the signal and I feel certain it is a quarter. I gouge a hole in the bottom of the ocean with my scoop and shake the sand through the sieve holes as I bring it to the surface. The ambient light and the moonlight are enough to spot the quarter in the shells. I pluck it from the scoop and I put it in my nail apron. How many thousands of quarters have I found? Is it really worth my time to scoop quarters? If I knew for sure it was a quarter, would I scoop it or leave it on the ocean bottom? There is no answer, for on a slow day I gladly scoop the quarter and on a day full of targets I hate quarters...and dimes and pennies. Nickels sound like gold so I don't hate them. If a gold ring is very large and alloyed with copper it will sound like a penny...so I rethink pennies. I mostly hate pennies.

I swing and get another target, a softer sound. In a minute I see a gold colored ear ring in the scoop. I hold it in my hand and I can tell it is not gold.

Each swing brings a new target and because the hole is small I dig it all. My nail apron is showing a bulge from the coins. Then I get a cell phone; the new junk to lose on the beach. Then I find an encrusted CO_2 cartridge, maybe from a paintball gun.

The next target is mid-tone and sounds interesting. I scoop once, twice and on the third scoop the sound disappears from the hole. When the scoop is out of the water I can't make out the target in the bottom. I am tunnel focused. There are a lot of shells in the scoop. I switch on the light on the brim of my baseball cap. My light and eyes scan the depths of the scoop. A small fish pings off of my knee. Are the small fish attracted to the light? Will they bring the bigger fish with piranha teeth?

I begin digging through the shells, pulling out the bigger shells first. At last, I see the small oblong fishing weight. I frown. I have to touch it. It is lead. I will get lead poisoning. The Romans went crazy from lead plumbing. Are the fish going crazy from all the lead in the ocean? Is there fish dementia? I put the lead weight in the nail apron. Maybe the parts per million won't kill me. Maybe eventually I will say strange things to the nurses. Will the forensics experts be able to trace my bizarre behavior back to the lead weights?

As I drop the scoop back into the water the light from my cap is on the water. Baitfish are everywhere tonight. I hurriedly click the light off.

I glance down the beach and see the crane standing in a few inches of water. Is he afraid of the deeper water? Is he a coward crane or has evolution put wariness into the cranes genes? Perhaps way down deep, in the cranes brain, he knows something sinister swims in the deeper water at night, in the soft light. A small fish nibbles at the hair on my right foot and I kick at it.

I step deeper into the hole, chest deep. The black ocean owns everything below my nipples; I can only feel the warm water. My heart rate quickens. The front half of a minnow floats by with that dead eye look.

Twenty feet towards the sea the surface water begins to jiggle and once again the surface erupts with flying, dying fish. I try to ignore the melee.

Now there are targets everywhere, the coil is speaking about the signals, trying to tell me what they are. *Time to get picky.* I wait until I get a medium tone and then begin scooping. As I shake the scoop I wonder about the curiosity of sharks. Are they listening and smiling? Is the sound of shells banging in the stainless steel scoop a dinner bell sound? My eyes search the surface for fins. Are the sea predators finning slowly nearby, watching the small shells dropping out of the scoop holes, fascinated by the shells looking like snow as they fall into the darkening depths. My heart is beating loudly. Can they hear my heart? Can they smell the fear oozing out of my pores? A fish with some weight bumps my thigh. *Dammit!*

I head for shore. My heart is racing. I wade quickly, as quickly as one can wade with a metal detector in one hand and a long handled scoop in the other. Each step puts me closer to safety. As the depth decreases I pick up my knees and sprint for shore.

I stand on the beach and look back over the quiet water. *Dammit.*

I dump the remaining shells from my scoop onto the wet sand. A small gold wedding band shines in the loose darkness. I pick it up and feel the weight, the heaviness of gold.

The crane flies by just off shore, wings beating slowly, legs trailing.

I curse myself, for I know I am a coward.

I head for the campground and the box. I call my camper "the box".

I hesitate and look back, a final look. The crane has melded into the night. A silver wave shushes up the bank. The moon is still above and below me and I am trapped in the world between.

Night hunting is fun! I enjoy the warm summer nights; the lack of crowds, the quiet. There are few things better than turning on the light on my cap and seeing gold in the bottom of my scoop.

The extra low tides of new moon and full moon expose more beach to hunt.

Night hunting is also a time to be on guard. There are crazies and zombies out there. There might be the boogieman too.

Hunt in well lit areas. Hunt with a friend.

Take a look around before you dig.

One night on the beach the fog rolled in and I could not see five feet. If I would have bumped into someone I would have washed up in the next high tide.

Never get in the water if the blues are feeding on baitfish. Blues have fangs much like piranha and will slash at anything. Also, the sharks follow these huge schools of baitfish. During the day it is possible to see the black acres of baitfish moving down the beach and the lifeguards will direct everyone out of the water.

Be safe and enjoy the night hunt.

Summary of Past Years at Myrtle Beach

2008...Lots of Gold Rings from the Surf

2008 was the year of the surf. Almost all of the rings that I found came from the surf. There were holes in the surf; often multiple holes in one stretch of beach; dark blue beauties full of treasure.

The beach renourishment was completed the end of 2008. Also, tropical storm Hanna added massive amounts of sand to the beach.

2009...Lots of Sand, Very Few Gold Rings

In 2009 my world was turned upside down. The excitement of a signal in the headphones was no more. Myrtle Beach was dead. The renourishment program had done what it was supposed to do; ruin the metal detecting. They did this to ruin my life. I took it personally. How else can one take it?

I never envisioned the beach or surf being so desolate, so empty of targets to dig.

One day I got two nulls in forty minutes of detecting. No bottle caps, no pull tabs, no coins. Forty minutes of threshold hum; sensory deprivation.

I held out hope that maybe a hole would show up in the surf. And once in a great while something resembling a hole would appear. The ocean bottom would be sand, without shells or rocks or signals. There was far too much sand.

Myrtle Beach passed a new motorcycle helmet law effectively telling the motorcyclist they were no longer welcome, to take the noise and chaos of Bike Week someplace else. This really had little effect on my detecting. Motorcyclist do not frequent the beach but they do discourage families from coming down during Harley Bike Week and Black Bike Week. **Note**: This law enacted by Myrtle Beach was found to be illegal and the motorcyclists have returned to MB in 2011.

2009 was the year of new drops. I was looking for new drops. I found thirty-two gold rings, less than one gold ring every eleven days. I consistently found less than a dollar in change in four hours. My spirit was broken, my enthusiasm gone; my heart was no longer in it.

Enthusiasm and excitement are what metal detecting is all about. And the unexpected, the surprise, the Holy Kamoly, what is in the bottom of my scoop. Doing the ring dance.

I was spending a lot more time detecting the beach than the surf. My reasoning was that you can swing two or three times on the beach to every one swing in the surf. Under these horrible sanded-in conditions it becomes imperative to cover as much square footage as possible. I'd developed a defeatist attitude. I knew I wasn't going to find anything. I was flogging a dead horse and I was the horse.

My frustration led to anger. So many days would go by between gold ring finds that when a gold wedding band would show up I was not happy. Actually, I was pissed off. "Damn, where in the hell have you been?" There was no joy, no ring dance.

And then there was the incident. It was another day of very few signals when I saw all of the little V feather antennas sticking out of the sand. Mole crabs use their antennas to catch plankton. I dug into the sand and threw the sand up the beach. A bunch of mole crabs immediately dug back into the sand. I dug them out and threw them up the beach. They dug in. I dug them out and tossed them out on the beach. They dug in. I repeatedly dug them out and tossed them on the beach. I was torturing mole crabs. I needed counseling.

I remembered the days before I moved to Myrtle Beach when I drove four hours in the pre-morning darkness to greet the sunrise and the low tide. It was extremely hard not to drive twenty miles an hour over the speed limit. When I would get to the parking lot I would grab my detector and literally run out on the beach, put the headphones on, adjust the detector, and realize that I had nothing to dig with. I'd left my scoop in the van. Get out of my way, I'm going detecting!

Some of the beach, the area north of the 14th Ave. Pier, had a gazillion shells and made digging extremely hard. I would push and jump and wrestle and fight with the scoop just to get an inch of shells out of the way. It would take seven or eight painful scoops to dig a pull tab at eight inches. Worse yet, the renourishment had also brought in 50 caliber shells and bullets. The Minelab would find these at fifteen plus inches. It took a Herculean effort to dig these relics from WWII. I really hated this section of beach, the shells, and the bullets. Forget the scoop or shovel, I needed a pickax. Any treasure hunter that needs to use a pickax also needs a burro. They allow horses on the beach in the winter, and burros' kind of look like horses. They're cousins.

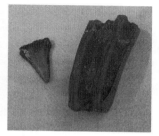

If there was an upside to the renourishment it came in the form of sharks teeth and fossils in the shell beds. I frequently found fossilized horse teeth and great white sharks teeth (over 1-1/2" long).

My carbon footprint was getting larger. I was doing a lot more driving to different beaches. I did this to save my sanity. The newness of a different beach gave me some hope. This can be frustrating as well, if one drives an hour to another beach and finds very little. And then the guilt sets in, knowing that you killed a little bit more of the earth and nothing was accomplished.

I did have one memorable day at Surfside Beach. The beach was eroded and fairly steep. I found three gold rings that blessed day. August 10, 2009

Which brings up one startling revelation; since the renourishment the holes in the surf are non-existent. There is just too much sand sloshing about. Almost all of my gold rings are now found on the beach, not in the surf.

Renourishment programs are reality. If Myrtle Beach erodes again they will renourish again. It is a never ending process. Myrtle Beach was sand enhanced in 1997-8 and then again in 2007-8. It took ten years to erode the beach enough to require renourishment.

On a scale of one to ten I would give 2009 a 1.75. My advice is to move away from renourished beaches. If you are a serious beach/surf detectorist pack up your stuff and leave the renourished beach in the rear view mirror. Don't dilly dally. Don't hang in there hoping that a storm will take all the renourishment sand off the beach. It may not happen for ten years or longer.

Can the serious gold hunter use *upcoming* renourishment projects as a signal that the sand on certain beaches has been depleted and would make for better detecting? I would think so.

- Renourishment programs are death sentences for serious beach/surf metal detectorists.
- Renourishment at MB slammed the door on surf hunting. The holes in the surf that got me close to the shell/rock/treasure layer no longer exist.
- Target *upcoming* renourishment projects for sand depleted beaches. Less sand equals more treasure.

2010...Lets Golf

2010 was better than 2009. I took some time off. I took up golf. Golf was my attempt to bring some balance to my life. I traded my frustration of metal detecting the beach for an entirely new frustration of trying to hit a golf ball.

So where are we today?

The winter of 2011 was very cold however it brought winds and new hope. One day the wind would come from the NE and the next it would come from the S. Sand began to move. By the first of April I had found twenty gold rings and Vince had nineteen. All of those rings came off the beach, none were found in the surf. Also, we used "run and gun" extensively. Most of the gold rings were not found at Myrtle Beach but on the beaches to the north and south.

The holes in the surf that were so prevalent in 2008 are a memory. Since the renourishment I never see the dark blue oval holes in the surf. I suspect that there is just too much sand and that it may take a few more years before enough sand migrates away from the beach before those holes will return. Occasionally I see washouts and runnels on the beach that hold big shells, rocks, and gold. In summary, I would say that slowly the metal detecting is improving.

The summer of 2011 has been typical of summer conditions; sanded-in. The other morning I detected for half a mile without so much as a null. The summer crowds have been good and I know that many rings have been lost. It is only a matter of time before a strong wind will blow open up the lid on the treasure chest.

Will conditions ever return to the glory days of 2008? I think so, but it may be years...or just a few days of 25 mph ENE wind.

2008...Running with the Big Dogs

January	0 gold rings	Beach Hunted
February	0 gold rings	Beach Hunted
March	0 gold rings	Beach Hunted

Started Surf Hunting

April	15 gold rings
May	17 gold rings
June	22 gold rings
July	14 gold rings
August	17 gold rings
September	9 gold rings
October	4 gold rings
November	13 gold rings &

1911 $5 gold coin

December	6 gold rings

I found no gold rings for the first three months of 2008. I blame this on my friend Vince. We hunted the beach frequently January through March but the beach was mostly sanded-in and we rarely found a dollar in change. As I recall Vince did find three gold rings on the beach during those three months.

I was hunting the beach because it is so much easier than hunting the surf in the winter. Winter is a time for wearing the wetsuit and if you hunt a lot it feels like you live in a wetsuit. After a while you hate the stinky wetsuit.

I justified not hunting the surf for a number of reasons. Vince was hunting the beach and finding a few good rings so I just kept swinging. And I was not seeing any holes in the surf.

At the end of March, Vince headed back to Pittsburgh. Suddenly, I was seeing holes in the surf. Why this sudden transformation? I have no earthly idea. Were the holes there and I just wasn't paying attention? Or did the fickle winds of late March open things up?

I have a theory. The winds of fall and spring are transitional, blowing from the north one day and the south the next. Holes in the surf seem to appear where waves come from two different directions and cross each other. I have experienced this a number of times…being in a hole and being slammed by waves from two distinct directions; comparable to being in a washing machine or dancing with a lonely fat lady that wants to lead.

The Awakening

In the first week of April, in the surf, I found five gold rings. By the end of April I'd found fifteen gold rings. I was on to something...something big. At last, I was tapping into the treasure zone. I happily put on my stinky wetsuit and drove around Myrtle Beach in my black Volkswagen.

The surf area was now taking on a different look. A substantial sandbar appeared approximately forty yards out from the low tide line. The area between the sandbar and the low tide line often had current and scooped out holes, holes filled with coins and gold. Sometimes the current was too strong and I ended up losing the battle. When the current was really moving it made it impossible to set the scoop and at times impossible to stand in one place without being blown downstream. It's extremely frustrating to hear targets and not be able to retrieve them. On severe current days I wondered if it would be possible to set a boat anchor upstream and repel down into the trough. That wouldn't fix the scoop setting problem though. I also wondered if I held the rope in my teeth and dropped down and fanned whether I could retrieve the gold.

For the most part I resigned myself to the fact that sometimes, fairly often, the surf was just not workable.

I had rings to post on the Ring Daddy page. Even with losing the first three months of the year my ring count started to climb. Would it be possible to catch some of these guys that had a big lead?

My eyes popped out on the end of springs at the beautiful pictures of gold rings that others were posting on the forum. My pictures were far less than dazzling. I began experimenting with my cameras macro mode and lighting. Slowly the ring pictures crept into the very nice range and occasionally I would get lucky with a dazzler photo. Natural light seemed best. I set up some white sheets of paper to make a light box and eliminate the shadows. The beauty of a digital camera is that you can take a hundred pictures of something and delete ninety-nine. In a round about way surf hunting forced me learn about macro photography.

I was surf hunting almost everyday and sometimes twice a day, if low tide fell in the morning and evening. I was finding gold rings. Diana and I were getting along well. The writing of my book about Jeb and Sludge was progressing. I was as happy as a dog with his head out the car window. Life was good, very good, and yet there was an uneasiness, a tension within me, that something bad was in the offing. Would it all come unraveled? Why did I feel this way...why? Damn it, why couldn't I just enjoy the moment without these feelings of doom? Is it that life is always changing and if you are at the end of the bell curve where life is super you realize that most of the bell curve is in the other direction? If I flip a coin six times and get six heads and I flip it a seventh time the odds are still 50/50 for another heads, and yet I know that sooner or later a tails is going to show up and then another and then another.

The local newspaper carried stories of the renourishment progress. For most of the year the renourishment was everywhere except the south end of Myrtle Beach, where I hunted most of the time. Diana and I drove to the renourished beaches and checked out the new sand and hunted for shells and sharks teeth. At one point, the dredgers packed up their equipment and went on an emergency mission. I smiled at the reprieve.

I was in denial. There was new sand to the north and south but it had not arrived where I hunted. It was not reality, yet. But really, how bad could it be? One good storm and all of the new thirty million dollar sand might be a memory.

Analyzing Success

As a young man I enjoyed fishing in Colorado. I subscribed to all of the outdoor magazines in hopes of learning to catch more fish. The March 1965 Sports Afield magazine had an article, "Fifty Trophy Trout" by Col. Dave Harbour. The magazine was thirty five cents then.

Col. Dave Harbour compiled all the information he could get on fifty trophy trout caught in public Colorado waters; what the trout was caught on, date, location, type of trout and of course, the angler. This information was put into a spreadsheet.

Certain things became evident from this information. One was the fact that some of the anglers caught more than one trophy trout in one season. Two, was the fact that huge trout are cannibalistic in nature and were caught on lures that resembled small fish. Three, was the fact that many of the fish came from the same body of water in Colorado, Lake John.

I was stunned. Holy tomato paste! It was possible to use statistics to catch big trout. There have been very few revelations in my life of this magnitude. I've never looked at things the same way, mostly because my eyes are still glazed over.

Today, quite a few metal detectorists keep track of their finds in some sort of spreadsheet or at least take pictures of their trophies and use a tag underneath to put the date, weight, and other information.

Let me encourage you to keep a journal, blog, scrap-
book, spreadsheet, or a CD with all of your pictures of your
trophies. This history will reveal some interesting things.

Data Mining the 2008 Season

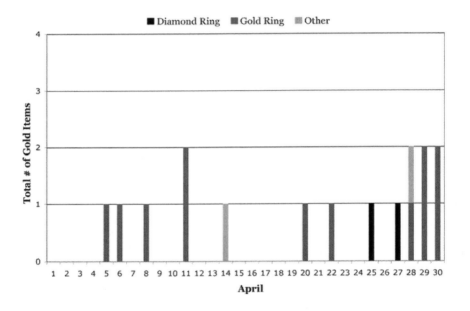

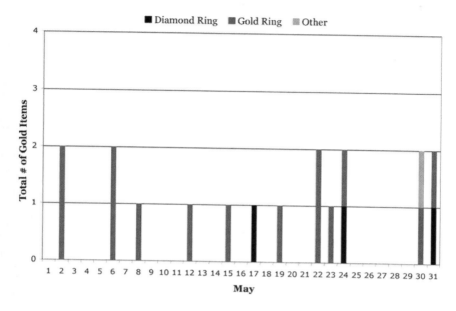

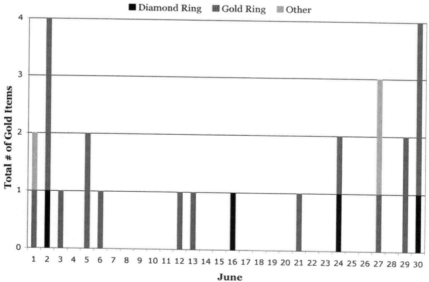

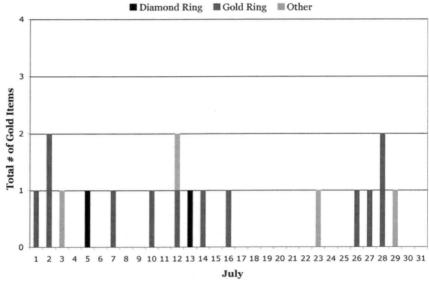

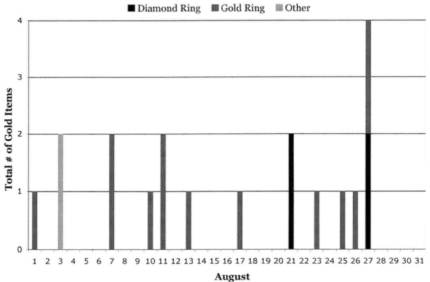

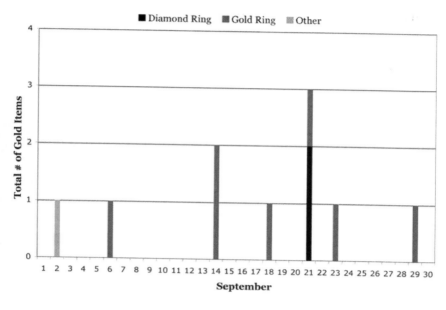

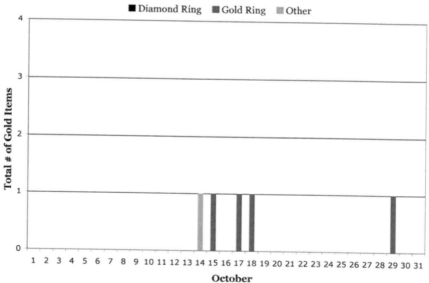

Gold Beneath the Waves

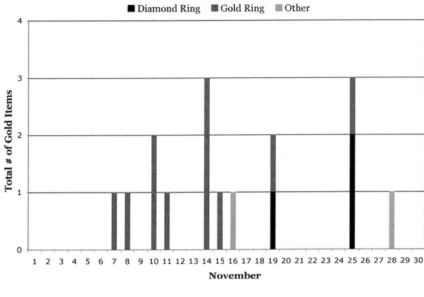

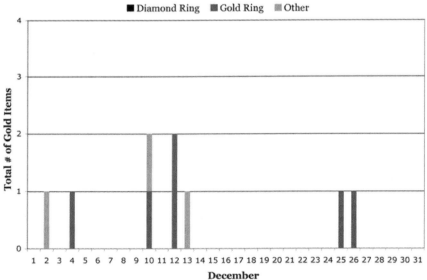

The charts show that:

In the nine months, 274 days, I found gold on 93 days or 1/3 of the days.

There was a total of 134 gold items found. 117 were gold rings or 87.3% of the total. 17 of the gold finds were bracelets, chains, earrings, or pendants or 12.7% of the total. I was almost 7 times as likely to find a gold ring as any other type of gold find.

On three occasions I found 4 gold rings, twice I found 3 gold rings, 22 times I found 2 gold rings. Therefore, 62 gold rings were found in 27 multiple gold ring days. 55 times I found one gold ring.

• *Gold Rings Come in Bunches!!* More gold rings were found on multiple gold ring days than on single gold ring days. When conditions are right to find one gold ring the chances are very high of finding more than one gold ring.

• Just as one will often find more than one gold ring in a day, one will have periods of feast and famine. If one were to graph the productive and unproductive periods it would appear as mountains and valleys.

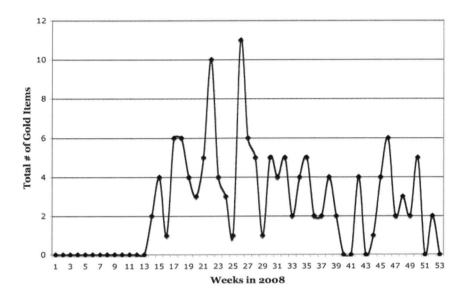

There were five extended periods of time, more than one week, where no gold was found, all of them after Sept. 6th. Tropical Storm Hanna hit on Sept. 6th with 70 mph winds and brought a huge amount of sand into the beach/surf area. It is my opinion that TS Hanna brought more sand onto the beach than the 2007-08 beach renourishment project.

April through August, the least amount of gold rings for a month was 14 and the average pre-TS Hanna was 17 gold rings per month.

In September I found 9 gold rings and in October I found 4 gold rings. I bounced back in November with 13 and finished December with 6 gold rings.

Post-TS Hanna average was 8 gold rings per month.

Out of 117 gold rings only three are what I consider "trophy" rings (worth more than a $1000 retail). All of the trophy finds in 2008 came from the surf.

One ring was platinum and one platinum/gold.

In reviewing the "mess" pictures (all of the items found during each hunt) of the 2008 season a number of things slapped me alongside the head.

I found very few pull tabs or bottle caps in the surf.

Quarters were the most prevalent coin found in the surf, to the point of being a nuisance.

Sinkers and motel keys were often shown.

As I recall, none of the pictures showed 50 caliber shells or bullets. I often find 50 caliber shells and bullets on the beach, especially after the beach renourishment projects. I can only remember finding one 50 caliber bullet in the surf in all of the years I've surf hunted. I'm not sure if we can draw any conclusions from this, however for those people who insist that heavy items like sinkers, 50 caliber bullets, and gold rings move around a lot I would say that 50 caliber bullets placed on the beach never move into the surf area. Never. At least not at Myrtle Beach.

- Wedding bands are the most abundant gold ring at MB.

- The average weight of a gold ring found at MB is 6-7 grams.

- Only five percent of the gold rings found at MB are class rings (a very low percentage). MB is not known as a Spring Break beach.

- Eleven percent of the rings had diamonds, albeit some were micro-diamonds.

• June was the best detecting month of 2008, 22 gold rings were found, followed by May and August with 17 each.

• Twenty-seven rings (23% of total) were less than 2 grams.

OK, this is just my gold rings for 2008.

What if you could find an even larger number of gold rings to analyze?

The Ring Daddy Page on the Surf and Sand forum under The Treasure Depot (my favorite website) has a huge number of rings to gawk at.

Just as some anglers catch lunker trout regularly, it is quite easy to see that some of the diehard detectorists consistently find large numbers of gold rings year after year. Many of these folks are retired...but there are also some weekend warriors that do extremely well. One Florida weekend warrior averages seventy gold rings per year. That in itself is pretty impressive until you realize that this is just the gold rings and does not include all the other gold items he finds. I'd have a conniption fit if I found that much gold just hunting on the weekends.

Luck plays little part in finding gold on the beach or in the surf. You get lucky when you use the right equipment, put yourself in the right spot, and keep swinging.

Florida seems to be the most popular state to hunt. Water temperatures that have people in the water almost year round are a factor in how many gold rings are lost and found. Myrtle Beach has comfortable water temperatures from mid-May to October, a much shorter season than southern Florida.

What else can we learn from Ring Daddy?

From the pictures of the detectorists we can generally say that we are a motley looking crew. Most of us would not be on the cover of GQ.

How about killer rings, the dazzlers, the ones that require sunglasses, the ones with quality diamonds? Out of the 499 gold rings found by the top five Ring Daddies in 2008 only twelve or thirteen would fit my criteria for killer rings, less than three percent.

Is it possible to tell the percentage of men's to women's rings recovered? Plain wedding bands make this a guess because quite a few women wear plain wedding bands. Also, too many of the rings could be worn by either men or women.

What is the percentage of class rings found? 34 out of 499 or only 7%.

Keeping Your Own Journal or Spreadsheet

We have worked with the major components of ring finds but there is other information, some of which might be vital in discovering what works where you detect.

- Wind and wave direction
- Neap or new/full moon tide
- Surf or beach find
- Location: physical address or GPS
- Section of the beach found; upper, lower, mid-beach
- Angle of the beach, steep or flat
- Were shells showing?
- Erosion or New Drop Find
- Hours hunted
- Was there was a specific reason for the find?
- Total number of targets found
- Type of detector used
- Who you hunted with.

Just as many trophy trout were caught out of Lake John so too there might be a location that is hot for finding gold rings under certain conditions. Data mine and find the treasure.

Bad Thinking and a Trip to Mount Failure

Much of our decision making is based on past experience. We relive our grand times over and over. If we find three gold rings in one day we will forever chisel a memory on the internal hard drive...and for the most part this is good. A three ring day represents a day of erosion and that we did our job efficiently; we located the erosion and we beat it up.

However, there are times that best be forgotten even though the outcome was good. Finding a diamond ring on a sanded-in beach will lead to faulty thinking, really bad thinking. How so?

In Psychology class, if we were paying attention, we came across a term called "intermittent reinforcement". It is a very powerful phenomenon. If something positive happens randomly we will have a tendency to try to replicate that event; a person winning on the slot machines is a perfect example. That person will try to win again, to feel that wonderful experience. A detectorist finding a gold ring on a sanded-in beach is another example. That detectorist will try to find another gold ring in this non-gold ring environment. This is broken thinking. The odds of finding a gold ring on a sanded-in beach are extremely small.

Summertime is notorious for giving up a gold ring now and then when conditions are absolutely horrible. Do not become a victim of summertime intermittent reinforcement!

Erosion is king and will always be king!! That random gold ring found on the sanded-in beach is a fluke. Do not be lured into thinking that you can replicate that experience. Doing so will lead to hundreds of fruitless hours searching the wrong areas. Wash the fluke gold ring from your memory banks.

Good beaches go bad. There will be a low tide or two that an area will be eroded and give up some gold rings and then the sand will cover everything up again. The success of those low tides will burn a pleasant memory in the brain and we will return time and time again, long after the conditions have turned bad. This leads to many wasted hours of swinging. Be brutal with your assessment of conditions and move on. *Yes, I know I got two gold rings out of here yesterday but today the beach is humped up again. I need to hunt elsewhere.*

Free yourself from bad detecting thinking. As you stand on the top of the beach, with all that energy about to be unleashed, pause and visit the cathedral of clear, honest thinking. "If there is erosion here I will stay and fight the good fight. If not, I will pick up and leave. I will put the odds on my side and find the gold."

A Trip to Mount Failure

We not only learn by success but by failure. Failure is good. Are you daft? Most of us don't like to think about our failures. We fill out little minds with pleasant memories of gold rings and chains. We bury the memory of hours of empty swinging. And yet, if we are honest, we need to visit Mount Failure which is slightly taller than Everest.

Even in my best year, 2008, I only found gold on one third of the days. Two thirds of the time I came away with a pouch full of non-gold items.

Could I have done better? Yes!

The renourishment (the artificially sand impregnated beach) ruined my detecting world but it also pushed me to hunt differently. I didn't want to hunt differently. I wanted things to stay the same. I wanted to go out and find a nice dark blue hole in the surf full of treasure and pillage and plunder it. That was the way to get the gold and that was the way I was going to do it regardless of how ineffective it was. I was full of the stupids and failure.

After failing so many hundreds of times in 2009-10 it occurred to me that I was the problem. I wanted what I wanted and I did not want to change. Even though I think of myself as a fairly open minded, flexible individual the reality was that I was Mr. Concrete Head. It sometimes takes a jackhammer to make me think differently.

Gradually, at the speed of a Slinky going up the stairs, I began to see that the areas I normally hunted were a waste of time unless conditions were absolutely perfect. However, if I explored the beaches to the north and south I often scored. I simply needed to expand my world.

I would have never invented Run and Gun if it were not for failure. Thanks failure. You're the best!

Hanna and the Attitude Phenomena

On September 6th 2008, tropical storm Hanna, with seventy mile an hour winds, came to Myrtle Beach in the early morning hours.

I could not sleep with the wind rumbling the roof of the camper. It was not worry of the storm that kept me awake but anticipation of the beach erosion that would surely take place. There would be gold rings and chains and bracelets lying on top of the sand. Thousands of coins would be exposed; silver coins, barber dimes, mercury dimes, flying eagle quarters, silver dollars, buried deep in the sand would suddenly be within reach of my metal detector.

Should I take two, maybe three nail aprons? Would it really happen this time?

Gold and platinum rings would make my nail apron look like chipmunk cheeks. I tossed and turned and listened to tropical storm Hanna.

Here is my account from my blog on September 6th.

TS Hanna pummeled MB hard from 11:30 till about 12:30 making the trailer roof rumble. And then it got quiet for twenty minutes and then a large gust rattled the roof but with a different rumble. Then it was intermittent gust rumblings. I could tell the wind was from a different direction. I slept fitfully and was glad when 5:30 came so I could get up. The rain and the wind was gone, the clouds sprinted across the late night time sky going north. At 6:15, in the predawn darkness, I left the car and headed through the dunes to the beach. Something was wrong. I had to walk up hill through the opening in the dunes. The dunes were massively sanded-in. I started chuckling as I got on the beach. There in the dark was one of the boxes used by the lifeguards and it was half buried in sand. The beach chairs were buried in sand. I switched on the Excaliber and wandered back and forth to the low tide line. Nothing. Not a peep. Hanna had done its damage...it had sanded-in the beach, as sanded-in as I have ever seen. Mountains of new sand. Hanna had accomplished in one night what the 30 million dollar renourishment program took months to do. What a hoot!! Now, I thought about all of the excited detectorists hitting the beach with wild expectations of wheelbarrows of loot, only to find sand and more sand.

At 6:30 I eased into the surf. The sandbar was breaking the waves nicely and making it workable. My first target was a silver ring. Green coins started to find their way into my pouch. And finally I heard that nice wholesome, I am not a pull tab, sound. Out comes a class ring. My first gold ring in ten days of hunting the surf and beach.

The waves grew large and ran me out. I tried the upper beach but could only wrestle up a few coins.

Here is the 14K class ring. 9.1 grams. So Hanna gave me a hole in the surf and massively sanded-in the beach. I know where I will be this evening.

Chalk up another storm that added sand rather than took it away.

After this storm my gold ring numbers plummeted. In September, I found only nine gold rings. I had been averaging 17 gold rings per month. Nine gold rings ruined my average. I blamed Hanna. I loathed what she had done to the beach. Sand everywhere. She was ruining my life and slowing my numbers on the Ring Daddy Page.

More importantly, this slow down in my gold numbers affected my psyche. I would walk out on the beach with a defeatist attitude. I knew I would not find a gold ring...and for some inexplicable reason I would not.

I would look at the beach everyday and see sand...horrible sand, sand that was piled far too deep to find anything. I was trying different spots up and down Myrtle Beach. They all seemed to be the same, very unproductive in my eyes. But I was slogging, my enthusiasm was gone.

On September 29th I found a gold ring on the beach.

On October 10th I recognized a guy in the surf that I had met before. He was busily digging targets and did not come out as I swung on by. The next day he was at the same spot and came out. His name was Phil and he was down for two weeks from Ohio. He asked me how I had been doing and I explained that Hanna had sanded-in the beach and I couldn't find anything. He gave me a funny look.

"You're kidding, right."

"Nope, I haven't found a gold ring in twelve days."

Phil just shook his head. "I've been doing real well. I just found a one carat diamond ring a couple of nights ago."

I said, "That's a better ring than anything I have found all year and I've found ninety four gold rings since April 1st."

"It really hasn't sunk in yet," he said still talking about his diamond ring.

When we parted ways I just chalked it up to luck that he had gotten that diamond ring. After all I was Foiled Again Jim.

In the next few days we kept running into each other on the beach and in the surf. He continued to find gold rings with his DFX and Beach Hunter ID. At last he confided in me that he had found 13 gold rings in 11 days. I was shocked and hurt. I felt as though someone had punched me in the stomach or possibly lower.

How could this be? It did not make any sense. I put in my time. I had better equipment. I wanted to take my detector, smash it against a palm tree and then scream at the parts lying on the ground, "Find something you ill begotten piece of ....!!" I hate to be beat and I didn't get beat, I got stomped.

Phil told me he had found eleven of the gold rings on the beach and two in the water. He had hunted every low tide about three hours. He was hunting the same areas that I hunted.

The last day that Phil was at Myrtle Beach, his wife, Wendi, came down and showed me the gold rings. There were two rings that matched or were better than any rings I had found all year. There was also a huge class ring, easily more than 20 grams.

What was the difference? How could this happen?

I talked with Phil Alexander from Shallotte, NC about this. He said the same thing happened when he went to Daytona Beach. He hunted as a man possessed. He was full of enthusiasm and eager to hit the beach. He slaughtered the locals.

In the final analysis, Phil from Ohio had no preconceived ideas about how badly the beach was sanded-in. He had a sense of urgency; all he knew was he only had two weeks to find the gold. He had dreamed about this vacation. He was strung tight. He hit the beach swinging and he is a very good detectorist.

Another factor that was just as important as his pants on fire enthusiasm was the fact that he mainly hunted the beach. I was prejudiced. I was successful detecting the surf before the renourishment and TS Hannah. I was surf hunting when I should have been beach hunting. I had defeated myself. I was defeated by faulty thinking. As Pogo said, "I have met the enemy and he is us."

Attitude! It all comes down to enthusiasm and being in sync with current conditions.

I needed a good swift kick in the attitude and Phil gave it to me. Thanks Phil.

Better Gold

In 2008, Myrtle Beach was being transformed from eroded beaches to mega-sanded-in beaches by the renourishment program and Tropical Storm Hanna.

This had an extremely detrimental effect for those of us that detect at Myrtle Beach.

As the huge pipes moved daily down the beach and buried more and more of the treasure I likewise moved down the beach, staying ahead of the new mountains of sand.

This meant that I was no longer walking or riding my bike across Ocean Blvd and detecting. I found myself driving further and further from the KOA campground where I lived.

Now, at first I was angry about losing more and more of the beach and having to drive to detect, but then something strange and wonderful started to take place; I was finding better gold.

The area that I normally would hunt is a strip of nice motels, nice but not grandiose. The new areas that I was detecting had nicer motels and clearly better clientele. The folks along this stretch of new beach were losing better jewelry, sparkly rings and 18K gold chains.

Rings 92,110, 116, and 117 are some of my best finds of the year and they came from a stretch of beach that I would not normally hunt.

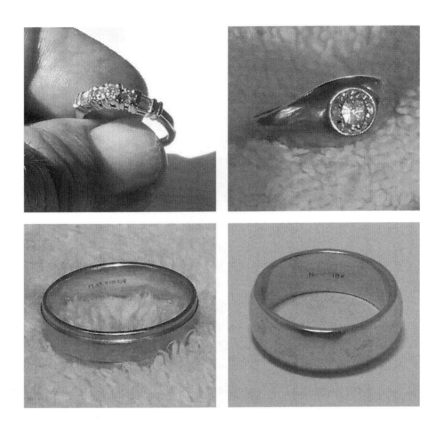

In November this same stretch of beach gave me a surprise, one of the things on my detecting wish list that I thought I would never, ever find.

The day was dreary and cool and so was my mood for it had been a while since I had found a decent hole to plunder. From atop the beach I studied the low tide surf and could see an area where the waves came smooth across the sandbar and then found new life, bouncing up and down, a clear indication of a hole. The hole was the size of a living room, no larger.

Now this section of beach is different beneath the sand. Where the sand has been removed by the waves and current, the bottom is spongy, black, smelly peat. The coins and gold have come to rest on this peat layer. Some of the coins are embedded in the first couple of inches of peat and are extremely hard to retrieve. Each clod of spongy peat must be broken apart to get to the black coin.

Decked out in my wetsuit I waded into the navel deep water and immediately picked up a few coins. I was cussing the peat under my breath as I broke the peat apart in the scoop with my hand and finally found another black coin. The black coins hide in this mess in your scoop. The next signal was a mellow mid-tone and I pushed the stainless steel scoop into the spongy bottom and broke loose another piece of peat. What a pain! After bringing the black chunk to the surface I had nothing. The signal had moved away from me. I set up again and took out some more black bottom. The scoop cleared the water and I stood looking at gold. I reached in and pulled the gold chain from the scoop. A gold bezel hung from the chain. The bezel was broken but still held the coin; a gold 1911 five dollar gold piece. *Could it be? Was it fake? Did it have "copy" stamped on it someplace? It's probably some cheap piece of junk.* I felt the weight of the chain and bezel and was sure it was gold. *Maybe it's real.*

The next day, at the local coin shop, the owner con-firmed that the gold coin was indeed real.

The realization was slow in coming to me. Beaches with huge glistening new twenty story expensive motels have better gold lost in front of them.

In saying this, let me emphasize the necessity of beach erosion or a hole in the surf. Detecting a hole in the surf in front of a rundown, beat up shack of a motel is far, far better than detecting in front of the Ritz-Carlton with no erosion.

Trophy Rings

Birds of a feather flock together. My mom would use this quote when explaining that bad people hang together and I should stay away from Eddie Haskell type people. As life progressed I found that this quote held true for more than just bad people. It was all about metal detecting.

The beach sorts out heavy weight objects and light-weight objects. Pull tabs and bottle caps flock together in old runnels on the beach. I seldom find lightweight objects in the surf.

A very loose generality is that women lose their gold rings at the top of the beach and men lose theirs lower on the beach and in the surf.

Interesting Facts:

My top three trophy rings were women's rings. Like, duh! Women wear the big diamonds. One is platinum and the other two are 14K gold.

Two were found near the top of the beach and one was found at mid-beach.

None of these top three rings were found at Myrtle Beach, where I hunt 90% of the time.

My two best trophy rings were found within 100 yards of each other (flocked together).

Both of these rings were found within six months of each other in 2011. One was found in a highly eroded area (wintertime) and the other was found when the beach was sanded-in (summertime) and had to be a new drop.

The ring on the left and the center ring were found within 100 yards of each other!

What can I really take away from this information? The most jolting revelation is that none of the three rings were found at MB, where I hunt 90% of the time. If I am hunting for trophy rings I am spending far too much time hunting the wrong beach.

The next revelation is that all three trophy rings were found on the upper half of the beach, not in the surf or on the lower beach where I hunt most of the time. So not only am I hunting the wrong beach, I am hunting the wrong areas of the beach...or so it would seem.

Should you hunt trophy rings or should you just hunt gold and be happy when a trophy ring shows up?

The answer is in the sand.

I hunt erosion. That is where I can find gold consistently.

What if I hunted exclusively where I found my two best rings? Rarely is the beach eroded where I want it to be. I would be very bored and finding very little if I hunted this one area only. Is it good to check this area regularly? Yep. And if it shows signs of erosion I will beat it up. If it is sanded-in I will go on down the road. The trophy rings will be there another day.

Cherry Picking or Going for the Gold

I love finding a hole in the surf and digging a jillion targets, most being one-scoopers. The problem is there are too many dimes and quarters.

Last winter the upper beach eroded leaving a three foot drop off to the lower beach. I found 175 coins and no jewelry that day. Pennies were the most prevalent coin.

Jason Reep from Tennessee was on the beach after Hurricane Ophelia. He said that you did not need a metal detector; there were visible clad coins everywhere.

The three scenarios above are situations where you have too many targets and not enough time.

Can you have too many targets? Absolutely!

There have been a number of articles in treasure magazines about the use of discrimination to increase the amount of gold found. Basically the writers say that one should not dig any items that could be identified as non-gold thus making the best use of one's time.

I agree with this premise only because I have dug a zillion targets.

A newbie detectorist out on the sand is happy with any target. It is fun to dig coins and silver rings. And after all isn't that what we are after; a fine adventure out on the beach or wading in the surf, a time of zoning out, enjoying the place and day as much as the finds. I often think of fishing for brook trout high in the Colorado Rockies. A brook trout is a beautifully decorated small trout found in the highest of places, tiny lakes, blue jewels fed by glaciers, surrounded by summer wildflowers. A ten inch brookie is a nice fish. I will never catch a four pound brook trout from such a lake and yet there is a heady joy in the experience. I will backpack miles into the wilderness to be in that place and time.

Many detectorists seek that nirvana quality experience and are rewarded with a day outdoors immersed in a hunt for treasure. And that is enough.

There are others who hunt with a passion to find the most, the best of finds, and to put bread on the table. They push the envelope of what is possible. In many ways they are not quite right. They live and die by what they find. They lie awake at night listening to the wind, visualizing large waves stripping the sand from the beach. They pour over old maps to see where the old motels and piers once were. They lose interest in a conversation that is not related in some way to beach detecting. They eat a complex carbohydrate meal before going onto the beach. They are constantly thinking of ways to improve their equipment and their expertise. They tie themselves to palm trees waiting for the hurricane to subside so they can be the first ones on the beach. In a howling windstorm they wear a parka with a hood and walk backwards into the wind. This is not a hobby for those obsessed, addicted, all up in it, gold finding junkies. Gold and platinum rings are the crack cocaine that drives these detectorists.

Patience is not a virtue, it's a waste of time...Damon Conlan.

Time; it is so precious and if we misuse it we don't achieve what is possible. One detectorist/writer used the scenario of a beach that allowed detecting only on the day after Labor Day. It was crucial to detect smart to get the most gold. Those who dug dimes at a foot have thrown away precious minutes, hours, and ultimately, a chance for more gold. *In the end, those that target the gold take home the gold.*

Every hunt is a gold hunt for some of us.

If one is going for the gold and only the gold, then metal detecting sounds differently in the headphones. All items found that are not gold or platinum are a time consuming nuisance. One cherry picks as best one can.

I was taught to dig all non-ferrous targets. If you are a gold hunter this is wrong, very, very wrong. It is also a very hard habit to break. It is probably easier to quit smoking than to quit digging all targets.

How to Discriminate...It's What You Don't Dig

Gold rings come in all shapes and sizes. Small gold rings will sound like foil. Really large 10K gold rings and rings alloyed with silver will sound like pennies. The most commonly found gold ring at MB is a gold wedding band of approximately 6-7 grams. These will be mid-tones and show in the middle of the screen (Minelab Explorer).

We know that only one in seven gold items is something other than a gold ring. The vast majority of these will also range from a barely audible foil sound for a gold chain or very small diamond pendant to a large gold pendant that may be alloyed with silver and give a penny sound.

Sounds are the most common way that a detector will give you some indication of what lies beneath the sand. Next, in line are detectors that give a visual readout on a screen along with a sound like the Minelab Explorer or have a digital meter like the one that can be added to the Minelab Sovereign.

Dwain Patrick tested 70 gold items with his Explorer and found only three rings that fell in the penny zone (4.3%). No gold items showed up in the quarter/dime region.

I tested 116 gold rings with the Sovereign and the digital meter. The meter was set up using a quarter at 550. A quarter or a dime would read 550 and a penny would read 539. I found one gold/silver ring that came in the quarter/dime number (550). I found one large 14K two tone wedding band that came in at 540. I suspect that the white gold part is alloyed with silver. I had six that fell between 528 and 537.

Using the Sov meter I could have eliminated digging quarters, dimes, and many of the pennies and only missed two gold rings out of 116.

Coins

So you are flying in on the targets in that hole, digging like a madman, shaking that scoop, filling the pouch and working as a man possessed.

Let's step back and ponder for a moment. Is there a better way to put the gold in the pouch?

On June 30th of 2008, in the surf, I dug 133 targets in the four hours of low tide. Most were one-scoopers. Many were loud, high sounds; obvious dimes and quarters. Sixty percent of the targets dug that day were dimes and quarters. Personally I do not like dimes and quarters. In fact, just to be frank, I hate coins. Coins in America, unless they are old, are pretty worthless. Canadian detectorists are blessed with loonies and toonies; one and two dollar coins. On the treasure forums I see some of the Canadian detectorists get over fifty dollars in coins in a hunt. That day in June I found over fifteen dollars in coins; coins that I hate.

Myrtle Beach has been renourished twice, burying all the old silver coins beneath mountains of sand and shells. It is a rare event when I find a silver coin.

If your beach has a history of giving up silver coins you may opt for the "dig it all" approach...or not, depending on how much value you place on old coins.

Normally, I average close to ten cents per coin found. It takes digging a hundred coins to get ten dollars. This is a horrendous waste of time for the gold ring hunter.

Is there a way around this "dig it all" mentality?

Pennies are the worst. Pre-1982 pennies were copper. The new pennies are zinc. Minelab detectors give a fairly high sound for copper pennies and on the Minelab Explorer screen are near the upper center. Zinc pennies are all over the screen because of how easily they corrode. I found a one year old zinc penny, 2010, that was half eaten away by the beach. It sounded close to a nickel.

Large gold rings, class rings come to mind, can be found in the same zone as pennies. This is because of the copper content. A large 10K gold class ring, say 20 grams, will have almost twelve grams of copper in the alloy. A few wedding bands will be found in the penny zone because they are alloyed with silver.

If one discriminates out pennies, sooner or later, one is going to miss a honker gold ring. Is digging all those pennies worth an occasional monster gold ring? Out of all 117 gold/platinum rings that I found in 2008 only two were monsters; one was 19 grams and the other was 26.4 grams. Both of these rings were found in the surf.

Pennies are found in massive numbers on the upper beach. In comparison the number of pennies found in the surf is minimal. *The best solution is to dig penny sounds in the surf and not dig penny sounds on the upper beach.*

Nickels fall right in the gold zone and I will gladly dig nickels. Nickels make up a very small percentage of the hated coins.

I loathe dimes and quarters. If I "dig it all" I will spend sixty percent of *my digging time* digging these pesky coins. Herein is an opportunity to be a better gold ring hunter. Quarters and dimes are at the top of the high sounds on a Minelab Explorer and reside in the very northeast part of the screen. Of the 186 items tested only one came into the dime/quarter zone. Be gone dimes and quarters. How do we accomplish this? If you have a very good ear, which I do not, you can simply not dig those blatant very high sounds.

Another possibility is to waterproof a Minelab Explorer which could be programmed to null over dimes and quarters. I don't see Minelab waterproofing their Explorers anytime soon so you will have to do it yourself.

Signals under signals. Twice that I know of, in all of my years of detecting, I have dug quarters and run the detector over the dug hole and picked up another signal that turned out to be a gold ring. So, yes, you may miss a gold ring if you don't dig every quarter or dime but the percentage is extremely small.

Here is the tradeoff. How many more gold rings would I have found if I had not dug every quarter, dime, and penny?

Pull tabs

For years I was puzzled by pull tabs. I never saw anyone throw their pull tabs down on the beach and yet there was always an abundance of the hateful little suckers. One day I dug a pull tab fairly close to one of the storm drains that empty out onto the beach and I became weak in the knees. I was having an epiphany. Was it possible? Yes, here was the answer. It made sense. The pull tab is tore from the can far, far away from the beach and finds its way onto the street. Here it lies until a rainstorm flushes it into the gutter and then the storm drain system. Early one morning the pull tab finds itself out on the beach. Here it lives happily until I find it and put it in my pouch to be taken home. Eventually it will be sent to Ronald McDonald House who recycles them. One can only speculate if the pull tabs then become cans and pull tabs again; pull tab cloning.

Pull tabs can be infuriating. A few years ago I dug over fifty pull tabs at Surfside Beach. (I had not invented Run and Gun yet). Almost all these pull tabs were found in a "fake" runnel. Pull tabs and bottle caps being lightweight move around until they find a low spot like this "fake" runnel. Birds of a feather flock together. A newly gouged out "real" runnel has large rocks and shells, treasure, and very few lightweight pieces of junk. It is imperative that the detectorist determine if the runnel is "real" (hunt the devil out of it) or "fake" (Run and Gun to a better spot).

Pull tabs are the most hated metal items that we dig. Pull tabs give off a mid-tone gold ring sound. They are gold ring imposters. They lie under the sand laughing, cruel demon laughter, knowing that some poor schmuck with a metal detector is going to mistake them for a gold ring. How should we deal with these deceitful, fraudulent targets? Is there a way to discriminate out pull tabs?

Absolutely! The easiest way to dig less pull tabs is to hunt erosion. Eroded areas are full of heavy items and have very few pull tabs. Sanded-in areas will produce huge amounts of pull tabs and bottle caps. If you are digging green quarters and nickels and sinkers and gold rings you will be digging very few pull tabs. Hunt Erosion! Wasn't that easy?

Bottle caps vary, but the majority has a distinct "burp" sound and do not have to be dug. Often, if one slows the swing, one can hear the null surrounding the signal and can identify the object as a bottle cap. If you run your sensitivity too high bottle caps will start to sound like good signals. Corona bottle caps are the hardest bottle caps to discriminate out.

Large targets are not gold rings...or any other gold item I can think of. Large targets are cans, large metal toys, chaise lounge chairs, metal rods that the life guards use for their flags, trash can lids, hub caps, and window trim.

The surf area is a discriminator of sorts; just by its nature it has far less trash than the beach. It has less pull tabs, bottle caps, lightweight items, and far less pennies. However, as pointed out in the Workable Conditions chapter there are many times that the surf area is not accessible.

Recently, I was told of another method to cherry pick. The detectorist stated he never digs deeper than three scoops. After a bit of thought I can see his point. The deepest gold ring I have ever gotten with a Minelab is close to 12". If you dig out 12+ inches of sand and you still do not have the target you can assume it is not a gold ring (the most prevalent gold item you will find). I personally would dig deeper if it is a mid or low tone signal.

Now, what if you only have one small hole in the surf to detect and can easily cover it in the allotted four hours of low tide? This is the time for "dig it all" and switching that VLF detector over to "all metal." A PI detector may help you get a few more deep targets in this situation.

• Cherry picking is for times when there are too many signals. On days of sparse signals "dig it all" and give the swinging arm a rest. Then again, if signals are sparse, what are you doing there? Run and Gun to a better location, to a place of erosion, to where the gold is buried.

Storm Chasers

Do you want the most fantastic beach metal detecting experience of your life? Chase a storm.

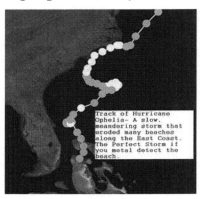

Track of Hurricane Ophelia- A slow, meandering storm that eroded many beaches along the East Coast. The Perfect Storm if you metal detect the beach.

In 2005 Hurricane Ophelia meandered and dawdled and staggered around like a drunk in the Atlantic and became one of the best storms for detectorists at Myrtle Beach in recent years. Somehow, I missed this one. I was probably mired eyeball deep in phone calls and emails in corporate America.

Jason Reep from Tennessee saw Ophelia for what she was; an opportunity to cash in on a naked beach. This is his account.

"It was insane. The beach was stripped of sand; it was down to the mud layer. I would fill my nail apron with coins and rings and take it up to the car and then come back and fill it up again and again. For two low tides I dug until I was too tired to dig." Jason paused and looked out to sea. "The third low tide brought all the sand back in. It was like it never happened."

"I got 10 or better rings, one heavy gold class ring and three other gold rings, if I remember correctly. I also got two buffalo nickels, some wheat pennies, a couple silver dimes, a silver Kennedy half, and 30 or 40 dollars in clad. The clad was lying everywhere, I would see a lot of it before I got to it with the detector."

So what does this tell us? It tells us we don't need a detector. It also points out that a slow moving hurricane just offshore will do a tremendous job of taking sand off the beach. Hurricane Ophelia was the perfect storm for metal detectorists with one major flaw. Ophelia was also the reason that Myrtle Beach was renourished in 2007-08.

On September 5th, 2004 Hurricane Frances hit the Ft. Pierce area with 105 mph winds. Twenty two days later Hurricane Jeanne took the identical path and hit the Ft. Pierce area with 120 mph winds. Side by side radar pictures show both storms in almost the exact same place off the Ft. Pierce coastline. Early information showed that the beach had suffered massive erosion. Beach access amounted to climbing down fallen trees that were on the edge of the 12' high cut.

Phil Alexander in Shallotte, NC realized the potential of these two storms and made the trip to Fort Pierce.

Upon setting foot on the beach Phil was dismayed that there were no other detectorists in sight. Doubts raced in and he thought that he must surely have made a mistake driving 620 miles to detect here. In a few moments those doubts were buried under the sand as the detector played target music in the headphones. In two short days Phil found close to fifty dollars in change, twenty four dollars in silver coins, and twelve pieces of gold.

Not every storm yields positive results for beach metal detectorists; far from it. Do you want some of the worst beach metal detecting? Chase a storm.

Tropical Storm Hannah blasted into Myrtle Beach on September 6th, 2008 with 70 mph winds. Hannah added massive amounts of sand to the beach. This was just after most of MB had been renourished by the Army Corps of Engineers. The double whammy of tropical storm Hanna and the renourishment cut my gold ring count in half (even though I hunted areas that had not yet been renourished).

Hurricane Irene in 2011 also added sand in MB. However, further up the coast in NC, Rick Poole, discovered a portion of Onslow Beach that had upper beach erosion and for ten glorious days after Irene he dug gold and silver. The five items at the upper left are gold. The number of silver half dollars and quarters is incredible. Yes, there are still lots of old silver coins on east coast beaches, but it takes a storm to shake it loose. I love those old coins.

The point of the two examples of Hurricane Irene is to stress that the same storm can have totally different affects on different beaches depending on location and angle of the beach to the storm.

Be careful what you wish for. Hurricane Ophelia was a two edged sword; it gave detectorists some great detecting for two low tides but it also was a major factor in the decision to renourish MB. The renourishment sand at MB has affected the detecting negatively for the past three years and will continue to be a detriment to finding gold in the years to come.

Also, sometimes if the hurricane does enough damage the beaches will be closed and the beach will sand back in before anyone has a chance to detect.

Every storm brings the possibility of some beach erosion and some fantastic hunting.

Chase the storms and dig the gold and silver.

The Golden Ghosts

Twice, in 2008, while metal detecting in the surf, I saw small gold chains fall through the holes in my scoop. Neither one of these gold chains was the target that I was pursuing. They just happened to get in the way of the scoop.

Small gold chains are extremely hard for a metal detector to pick up. In early 2011 I found a small gold chain with a gold cross attached. The cross gave me the signal. One day as Vince and I were running from beach to beach we were discussing the lack of gold chains. I told him we needed to do some testing to see if he could pick up the small gold chain with his Explorer II.

I put the chain in a small plastic pouch and we went out to the beach.

After finding a clear spot I placed the plastic pouch with the chain on the sand. Note that the chain was bunched up in the bag. Vince swung across and got nothing. He went to "all metal" and got more nothing. He upped the sensitivity to the max and got even more nothing. He was in disbelief.

We took our new found knowledge and Vince's Explorer II up to Bob's place. Now, Bob is a gold nugget hunter and panner of gold flecks. He showed me some of his finds and we finally got around to showing him how the detector would not pick up the gold chain. Bob took a small gold nugget, approximately 1/8" in diameter, and ran it across the coil. The detector easily picked up the nugget out to a range of ¾ of an inch.

The chain in the picture below was the one that we could not pick up with a detector.

How many gold chains are out there? How many golden ghosts have fallen through my scoop before it reached the surface?

The Mystery of Old Coins and Class Rings

For several days and nights the coin tumbler had run almost non-stop. I pulled the plug and listened to the quiet. I did a mental sigh of relief. I put the last batch of silver coins in the plastic basket, washed them off, and dumped them onto the pile on the large white towel.

What a mess of coins! I promised myself never to let the coins build up like that again. But the summer had been good for metal detecting and cleaning coins was a lower priority.

The pennies took ages to sort out and then look through for "wheaties".

The pile was now all silver colored coins; nickels, dimes, and quarters. Over twelve hundred coins in all. I was eager to look for the silver quarters and dimes, pre-1964 coins. Coins minted after 1964 are garbage metal.

After sorting the dimes, quarters, and nickels into their piles I began another treasure hunt. I picked up eight or ten quarters and looked at the stack from the side. The edges of clad coins have a reddish tinge to them. True silver coins are silver in color and the edges stand out like the white part of an Oreo cookie. This process of looking for silver goes quickly. Then the dimes are inspected the same way.

One beat up silver quarter out of all those coins. How can this be?

In reviewing the 117 gold rings found in 2008 only five are class rings and the oldest was 1983. Where are the old class rings?

Hurricane Hazel hit the east coast in 1954 and instead of dampening the economy a building boom took place. Myrtle Beach became a major tourist town with many attractions and new motels.

All of this only deepens the mystery of why I have found very few silver coins and no old class rings. Surely they are there, buried beneath the beach.

Hurricane Ophelia in 2005 shed some light on the mystery. Jason Reep was a fortunate detectorist that hunted after Ophelia took the sand from the beach. For two low tides Jason found massive amounts of coins, some of them silver. Jason said that the beach was eroded down to the hardpan. Incredible! So yes, the silver coins and quite possibly the old class rings are still out there in the surf...at the lowest level, beneath the sand and the renourishment shell layer of 1997.

My conclusion is that the vast majority of coins and gold rings that I found in 2008 were in the top layer of the 1997 renourishment sand and shells and all were lost between 1997 and 2008. This is the reason for never finding any old silver or old gold rings.

The newest renourishment in 2008 has now added yet another new layer of shells atop the layer of shells that were already there. Just speculation: the coins and gold rings found in the future at Myrtle Beach will have been lost since the last renourishment and none will be old.

The artificial shell layers from the renourishment programs have buried the old treasure...until another Ophelia or a nor'easter sweeps the east coast and the bottom of the ocean glitters with silver and gold.

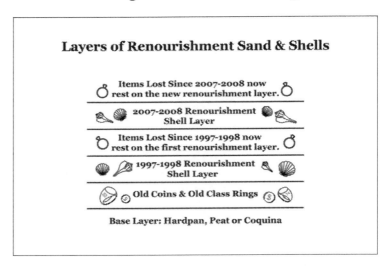

- The old silver and gold is still there, buried beneath the layers of shells brought in by the renourishment projects.

- Storms reveal the old silver and gold, but only for a moment. In a few tides the sand will once again bury the mercury dimes, standing liberty quarters and old gold rings. Hurricane Ophelia was the perfect storm.

- Just an opinion. The artwork on the old silver coins, the mercury dimes, the walking liberty half dollars, the seated liberty quarters, the barber coins are unmatched by any coin minted today. The old coins had depth, and contrast, and depicted beautiful ladies in flowing gowns and flying eagles. They were satisfying to look at again and again. And they were silver, real silver, coins that will never lose their value. These coins were from a time when a boy would gladly mow the neighbor's yard for a dime. A time when children said, "Yes sir," and "No sir." A time when a silver quarter had value for its beauty and the metal that was used to mint it. Hold a Walking Liberty half dollar in your hand and feel the heft of the rare heavy metal, gaze at the eagle taking to the air, then close your eyes and ride the silver winds into the past.

Beach History

Apache pier was a hundred yards to the NE. The shadows from the motels grew long. I kept swinging and hoping.

A man came off the top of the beach and angled toward me. I was sure I knew what he wanted and what would be said. It was always the same.

And so it began, as always. "Are you doing any good?" he asked.

"I found a few coins, pull tabs, bottle caps, and miscellaneous junk."

"Have you found any 50 caliber shells or bullets?"

I hesitated. He wasn't following the script. He was supposed to ask me, "What's the best thing you've ever found?"

"Uh, yeah, I've found three shells so far." I pulled one of the WWII shells out of my pouch to show the man.

"The reason I ask is that I teach history at the high school and I like to have artifacts to go along with my history lessons. I used to metal detect and had quite a few 50 caliber bullets and shells but I have given most of them away. I'd be willing to pay you a dollar a piece for them."

Wow, a teacher that really teaches history. "Here you go." I handed him the three brass shells. He offered to pay me again and I turned him down.

After we parted I kept detecting, swinging the coil, and wondering what it would have been like to have had a real history teacher.

In February of 2010 my friend, Vince, while detecting the beach found a monster 20 mm tank piercing shell. Basically, this looks like a stick of dynamite that one would put in a rifle. It is the shell at the top of the picture. The 20 mm shell was found after the 2008 renourishment of the beach and was probably dredged from the ocean bottom miles from shore.

The day after Vince found the shell we were in McDonalds and one of the local policemen said that the 20 mm cannons were mounted on planes during WWII.

The Google search began.

I have summarized to keep things short and tidy.

During WWII the US favored the 50 caliber shell. The 50 caliber is also referred to as 12.7mm.

20 mm cannons were installed on a handful of fighter planes and the B-29 Superfortress.

http://increte.110mb.com/tomfeise/8thusaaf/planes.htm

In 1940 the Myrtle Beach Air Force Base was established as a WWII training facility. Early training used the beaches and the area near Singletons Swash for target practice.

In 1941 the Army Air Corps expressed interest in using the base for pilot training and two concrete runways were constructed.

In March of 1942 the base was renamed Myrtle Beach General Bombing and Gunnery Range.

In 1944-45 the Myrtle Beach AAF performed coastal patrols, monitoring for German U-boats.

http://en.wikipedia.org/wiki/Myrtle_Beach_Air_Fo rce_Base

In early 1942 German U-boats took a heavy toll on ships off the east coast particularly the area off the Outer Banks. This area was nicknamed Torpedo Junction.

Cities along the east coast were asked to turn off their lights at night during WWII. The German U-boats were using the lighting from cities to backlight ships and make them easy targets. I ran across this fascinating article on line.

http://ncpedia.org/history/20th-Century/wwii-uboats

OK, we have established the fact that the 20 mm cannon was mounted on a number of fighter planes and that the Air Force monitored for U-boat activity off the coast. We also know that the renourishment dredging brought in sand miles from shore. We can easily speculate that the 20 mm shell was in the dredging. Was Vince's 20 mm shell used for target practice or is there, deep beneath the waves, a blizzard of fish swirling around a German U-boat with 20 mm holes in it?

In all of the years that I have hunted the beach I have only found two civil war bullets; three ringers. One was found at Folly Beach and the other was found at Holden Beach. Both of these beaches played a part in the civil war.

Some beaches are old, meaning they are rich in American history. Beach detectorists that frequent these beaches find that history; early American coins, Spanish coins, musket balls, pistol balls, cannonballs, and very old gold rings.

The things we find on the beach or in the surf are a reflection of who we are, a cross section of our society. Just as arrowheads and spear points found in fields after the earth has been plowed give us some insight into the past, the items found with a metal detector often make a historical connection.

The longer I metal detect the beach the more I become aware of how things in our society are changing. Not so many years ago I found a fair number of watches. Today, I rarely find a watch. People are using their cell phones to check the time. Now, cell phones are found quite frequently in the sand. I found two in one day last summer. And I find cell phone batteries.

Rings are no longer just gold and silver. Today I find titanium, stainless steel, tungsten carbide and other junk metal rings. Perhaps this is evidence of a weaker economy, a poorer country or maybe it is evidence of a new frugality, saving more, borrowing less, being more responsible with one's money.

The most common foreign coins found at Myrtle Beach are Canadian coins; dimes, quarters and an occasional loonie or toonie. These are usually lost in the winter by the large group of Canadians that are trying to escape the snow and cold up north. Other foreign coins come from many European countries and Russia. I suspect that most of these coins are lost by the large number of young people that come to Myrtle Beach for part-time summer employment.

Millions of years ago Myrtle Beach was quite different. Huge sharks, sixty feet long, called megalodons and forty-five feet long mosasaurus ruled the seas. Dinosaurs roamed the earth. As I comb the beach I'm not only metal detecting but also fossil hunting. My nicest find from the beach is a mammoth tooth. Last winter when the beach was badly eroded I found three megalodon teeth. I also have horse teeth, a mosasaurus tooth, a couple of pieces of ivory (from tusk), a pile of shark's teeth, whale vertebrae, and a box of bone fragments. Most fossilized bone fragments found on the beach are not in good enough shape or give enough information to identify the dinosaur.

Every fall there is a fossil show in Myrtle Beach that has a few fine folks from the Smithsonian Institute that will help identify your fossil finds. Be aware that most fossilized bone fragments are black. White bones are from KFC.

This is a great show for kids. They give away free sharks teeth and last year they had some people that helped the kids, young and old, wire wrap sharks teeth to make sharks tooth necklaces.

- From wooly mammoths to WWII tank piercing bullets to cell phones, the beach sand of Myrtle Beach is full of history.

- History is more than dates and men wearing wigs. Take a kid to the beach and let him find something old with a metal detector or have him find a Great White Sharks tooth and suddenly history is alive! How old is the fossil or the bullet or the encrusted coin?

Every time I unearth a WWII 50 caliber shell I think about the teacher with a passion for history and wish that I had been one of his students.

Surprise

The beach had horseshoe shaped holes between fingers of mounded sand. I was working each hole, wading into the naval deep water, plundering the treasure to be found and then hurrying over the hump to the next hole.

A couple, beautiful people, she with blonde hair and he with chiseled face, sat in those chopped off chaise lounge chairs atop the mound as I made my crossing to the next hole.

Whaaaa, whaaa. *Hmmm??? Pull tab. It has to be a pull tab up here on top of this mound. I know a pull tab when I hear one. Better check it though.*

I set my scoop and dug out a sizable chunk of sand. I swung over the hole. The target was in the pile of sand. I kicked the pile. Out of the sand a gold wedding band stood upright and rolled wheel-like for several feet, right in front of the couple. The woman's eyes got large, her mouth dropped open, and she pointed. The husband was looking elsewhere.

I snatched the ring from the beach, put it in my nail apron, and hurried on.

My legs and feet felt young and strong. I glanced around. There were too many people on the beach. I must control myself.

I waded into the water, pulled the gold ring from the nail pouch and washed it off. I held it where others could not see. The sun devilishly reflected off the gold and I closed my eyes.

I clenched my fist around the ring. I was in the middle of the high school cheerleading squad. I was the white guy without pom-poms. I moved with the black girls and chanted,

"Uhh, Ungowah,
Jim Brouwers got the power,
Sayin Uhh, ungowah,
Jim Brouwers got the power."

Ain't nothing like a good ring dance.

Competition and Claim Jumpers

Is there good competition? I know my friend Vince has made me a better detectorist. He pushes me to hang in there longer. If he finds a gold ring then it motivates me to concentrate more and think about what I need to be doing. I also know that if conditions are good to find one gold ring that there are others lurking about. If Vince finds two gold rings I start to mutter and look at the sky. I fester. My swing rate doubles. If Vince should find three gold rings while I still have none, I plot revenge. He will never make it back to the car.

Competition is good when I'm winning.

Recently (Feb. 2011) a detectorist on the Surf and Sand forum was very upset about his trip to Puerto Plata. He found very little and blamed it on having posted his finds from there in the past and claim jumpers ruined his spot.

And he very well may be right. He may have caused a gold rush to this resort.

Puerto Plata, from his trip pictures, looks like paradise. Beautiful turquoise water with nary a wave, where the well to do, wade and swim and lose their jewelry. Looks like detecting in a clear blue sky on a warm day. Yes, it is possible with advertising like this that Puerto Plata has seen much more competition.

Increased gold prices have also played a part in the present gold rush. After all, you just buy a metal detector, run out to the beach, and the gold just hops into your pouch. Nothing to it, so easy a cave man could do it.

It's been said that 10% of the fishermen catch 90% of the fish. I'd say this is true for metal detectorists also. Just as fishing guides know the lake and where the fish hang out, your better metal detectorists have a plan and a method. They have put in the hours and taken their lumps. They have learned from their bad days. They analyze what worked and what didn't. That elite 10% have their favorite spots, use the best equipment, do the research, work smart, and put in the time. The quote, "The harder I work, the luckier I get," is the motto of the best metal detectorists. The top 10% are all up into their detecting.

Now, if you have put in the time, worked hard and smart, should you shout to the world on the internet, "Hey, the gold is over here?"

I am like every detectorist in that I want to succeed. I spend way too much time thinking about that next gold ring. I am obsessed. I want it reeeal bad. I need my gold fix.

If the beach I am currently detecting is sanded-in and not producing and someone just down the road is killing it and giving out the location, I too will have to take a look. I too am a dirty, no good, sidewinder, claim jumper. I am your competition.

Working under the cloak of darkness, keeping a low profile, staying in the shadows, melting into the fog is a good idea if you have a favorite spot. I participate in the Surf and Sand forum but I never give out the location of where I make a find. I've also decided to have a "waiting period" after I make a find or two. Posting immediately of a great day in the surf on the internet alerts others that it might be time to plunder the beach. Posting a couple of days after the beach has again sanded-in or the hole disappeared insures that I don't find two or three folks working my claim. I don't want you stealing my gold.

Puerto Plata looks too easy. The water is too clear, the waves are too small, and the weather too nice. I am blue-green with envy.

This was my response on the forum.

Hmmmm...I guess I would be upset too...and since I've never been to someplace exotic and expensive to go metal detecting I can't really relate.

The pictures show a beautiful beach and ocean to swim in. I can't imagine such a place to metal detect. I doubt that I will ever have enough money to go to such a paradise.

Here at MB the beach has been renourished twice. The detecting is 100% dependent on conditions. 80% of the time conditions are bad to extremely bad. 10% of the time they are fair and 10% or less conditions are good.

The water viz is murky to disgusting brown 95% of the time. At times jellyfish are very plentiful and you will get stung on a regular basis. It is part of detecting here.

When the beach is sanded-in, it is sanded-in. It can be the middle of summer and you will be hard pressed to come up with a dollar in change.

The waves are normally three feet. You will get slammed around and beat up.

Kids will bother the hell out of you.

MB is twenty miles long and I will hunt from Holden Beach in NC to Pawleys Island, a fifty mile range.

This is called hunting. You only get what the conditions will give you.

We don't have loonies and toonies. We find pennies...lots of pennies and pull tabs and bottle caps and scrap aluminum that sounds real nice.

Sorry your metal detecting didn't work out.

There are much better places to metal detect than Myrtle Beach.

Do I fear the competition? Yes and no.

It takes a commitment to be a big dog surf/beach detectorist.

It also takes strength. Most people lack the strength to swing a metal detector in the water or on the beach for four hours or lack the strength to drag a heavy stainless steel scoop around, and then retrieve the target, digging into the ocean bottom and shaking the hugely heavy sand laden scoop until the penny is found.

It takes perseverance. How many pull tabs are you willing to dig before you give up; fifty, sixty?

It takes knowledge of beach/surf conditions.

Are you willing to go in the water knowing that you will be stung by jellyfish?

Are you willing to take a beating in the waves?

Do you have a wetsuit to wade the frigid waters of January?

Are you willing to wade the surf at two o'clock in the morning while listening to the music from Jaws running through your brain?

Does it bother you when crabs bite your feet?

Are you skittish when you step on a skate or flounder and they go wiggling out from under your feet or when a fish bangs into your legs?

Are you bullet-proof and impervious to cold winter rain and sultry, humid August heat?

How high is your tolerance for kids getting in your way and knocking into you with their wave boards? How high is your tolerance for adults that torture you with the same question over and over and over, "What's the best thing you've ever found?"

My competition seems to be dwindling. And yet there are a few individuals that are my competition. They know pain and suffering. And they know how to find gold.

Twice in the last four years I've found another detectorist in "my spot" and it ticked me off. There's a bunch of bad folks in this world. There are horse thieves and card sharks and gunslingers and cattle rustlers and stagecoach holdup guys and women that insist that you get a job. But there ain't nothing worse than a claim jumper.

Mistakes

Many years ago, in a land far away from the beach, there was a large field in the middle of the small town of Troutman, NC. I'd just gotten into metal detecting at the time.

After a few sessions of swinging I realized that the field had been detected many times. I did manage to eek out a few V nickels but no silver coins. But the field being close to home was a good place to spend an hour swinging my Tesoro.

My experience to this point was playgrounds, an old park, and this field. I was hunting coins...and had very little knowledge of other things metal that might show up.

It was late winter and the grass and weeds were ankle high.

I got a high signal and dug a few inches down to a rock. I still had a strong signal and suspected that the coin was below the rock. I worked around the rock with my small shovel and was a bit miffed at so much work to uncover a coin. After considerable effort I pulled the hugely heavy two liter Coke bottle sized rock from the ground and put it off to the side. *Dadgum, that rock is heavy!* It was all I could do to pull it from the hole. I put the coil in the hole. Nothing. Grrr. I swung around the edge of the hole and as I neared the rock I got a signal. It was the rock.

I'd read about hot rocks and how they would give you a signal. Armed with this tiny bit of knowledge I pushed the rock back in the hole, filled it in, and stomped it down with my boot.

Many months went by and I stumbled across an article about meteorites. As I read, a memory edged around the corner from the darkness. *Oh no, what have I done!*

The next day, as I drove past the field, I noted that the weeds were waist high. I would have to wait.

As with many things, we get caught up in the rush of life and the "maybe meteorite" fell off my radar screen. Besides, I'd been bitten by the beach detecting bug. The field and the meteorite could wait, it wasn't going anywhere.

In less time than it takes to eat a bowl of cereal the field was transformed into a shopping center.

* * * * *

I've always had beautiful, sculpted, strong, athletic feet. 10-1/2 EEEE's. Artists that do foot sculptures would swoon upon seeing my feet. I've never had this happen, but it could.

It's kind of a blur of misery, that first trip to Myrtle Beach. The six hour drive in the MG midget wouldn't have been nearly as bad had I been the driver. As the passenger I prayed constantly. My eyes were at the same height as the lug nuts on compact cars. The passenger side of a MG midget was an after thought or maybe no thought at all. The leg compartment narrows to the left, toward the center of the car. This is a good fit for someone with only a left leg.

Oops, I called it a car. It is not. It is a coffin with wheels. My Geo Metro was spacious and elegant in comparison.

We arrived in Myrtle Beach at sunup and picked the wrong pancake house to eat at. The pancakes were slightly less dense than concrete. My glass of water gave off a distinct odor. I took a sip and gagged. Beach water. I thought it was not possible to ruin breakfast but I was wrong.

The ocean looked like an ocean should look. Clear blue water.

Living in the NC Mountains, a place of eternal rain, fog, and moist dreariness, did not prepare me for the beach. Sunshine in the mountains is a rare event; they hold presidential elections more often. My skin was pale, an off white, eggshell perhaps.

I slathered on the sunscreen to my arms, chest, legs, face, everywhere except my feet. After four hours of blazing sunshine, I noted that my feet were red. Red rose's red. Scarlet letter red. Back at the hated MG I discovered that my feet would not fit in my shoes. My feet were growing exponentially. I wondered how much skin could stretch. These were not blisters; they were ponds of water under stretched taut screaming red skin.

A quick trip to Wally World to buy aloe with lidocaine. My head was throbbing and I was told that I had sun poisoning. I wasn't nauseous until I looked down at the red shoeboxes that were attached to my legs. My feet were now 12 F's. My toes were fused together and gave the appearance of Ball Park Franks. I was told that people died from sun poisoning. I hoped that was true and that it came soon.

I could not let anything touch my shoeboxes. Slight breezes were shock waves from a blow torch. Sleep was not possible. I could feel my pulse in my toenails. Massive doses of Ibuprophen helped ease the pain and lessened the screaming. Feet that scream are annoying.

I lived through the ride back to the mountains and on day five I could gently put on my shoes. I'd survived my first beach trip and had no intention of ever going back.

* * * * *

I had found a cremation tag on the beach and was describing the find in all its glory to Phil Alexander on the phone.

Phil finally got a word in edgewise, "Jim, did you find any small, heavy pieces of black metal when you found the tag?"

"I don't remember. Why?"

"Sometimes when they dump the ashes on the beach there are gold teeth in with the ashes. The gold teeth get melted into dark gray blobs and a lot of detectorists throw them in the trash."

After Phil hung up I thought about all the small dark gray metal blobs I'd thrown out in my beach detecting life.

Since Phil alerted me to this situation I have found two gold teeth on the beach. With a toothbrush and a small amount of elbow grease those black blobs become golden blobs.

Dental gold may be up to 18K.

* * * * *

I'd filled a pickle jar ¾ full of trinkets; gold and silver wannabe jewelry, mood rings, junk rings, ear rings, belly button dangles, and pendants of non-descript metal.

Cheryl Mahoney was having some friends stay at her place and they had two young kids. I thought it might be fun to share the "treasure" with the kids. Cheryl brought out a large blanket and put it on the living room floor and I dumped the pickle jar. The treasure hunt began as the kids sifted through the booty. I noticed Cheryl would occasionally bend over and pick out a piece. It was a fun evening.

A few weeks later Cheryl came by and handed me five pieces of silver jewelry she had plucked from the debris and then she said, "I ought to keep this one." She handed me a ring, shiny silver in color with a hundred little colored stones on the top. "Chintzy" would be a word with way too much class for this ring. Cracker Jacks had better looking rings. I said, "No way."

"It says 10K on the inside."

"You've got to be kidding."

"Nope. You need to be a bit more careful what you throw out."

Later as I looked through my magnifying glass I spotted the 10K...but I still could not believe it was gold.

Months later I weighed a few gold rings, this one included, and sent them off to the refinery. When I got the report from the refinery the weight of the 10K gold matched my figure.

Every year Cheryl Mahoney picks up a few gold items at yard/garage sales that are mistakenly thrown in with the costume jewelry.

Cheryl has spotted the almost microscopic markings on the ear ring clasp. "What do you want for this?" she'll ask, holding up the gold ear rings.

"Five bucks."

"I'll give you three."

The guy hesitates; shakes his head, and sighs, "Sure."

Now it's Cheryl's turn, "Are you sure you won't take two bucks?"

The guy chuckles. "Two bucks."

Gold is where you find it.

* * * * *

I'd listened to the threshold, that buzzing of bees far off across the field where the hives were, for far too long. I wanted quiet. I was sick of listening to the incessant hum for four hours every day. It was a form of torture. I'm in charge and I'll do it my way! And thus it came to pass that Jim turned down his threshold to where it was not audible. Take that!

I lived in blissful silence until I was interrupted by a signal. This went on for months and I was happier with the silence until...I was reading a post on the forum about listening to the threshold for the nulls and realized that I was no longer hearing nulls. *Hearing tiny nulls in the threshold is very important!*

At the very edge of a detectors discrimination is a layer where the detector says, "I don't know what this is," and will give a null. Sometimes the target is off to the side and other times it is buried at the maximum depth that the detector gets a return signal. If one is aware of these tiny blips in the threshold and returns the coil to the blip spot often one finds that it is not iron but a good target. Swinging faster can sometimes enhance the signal. Opening your mouth like you are yawning can also enhance the signal. I discovered this phenomenon one day as I was detecting/yawning. When in doubt, dig out a scoop of sand and swing again. Does it null or give a good target sound?

I've no way of knowing what the percentage is of good signals are found investigating tiny blips but I'll take a guess at 20%. I'm not talking about rechecking big, blatant iron signals; I'm talking about those subtle cut outs in the threshold.

Clive Clynick has written quite a few books on metal detecting and has made a study out of listening to threshold and using the correct sensitivity to get the most out of your detector. I highly recommend his books. Knowledge is power and more gold rings.

* * * * *

I was tired, so, so very tired. Zombie tired. I hurriedly put the Excaliber battery on charge and went into the other room.

Boomyow!

I ran back into the other room and found my Excaliber battery in pieces on the floor. *What in tarnation happened?* As I was picking up the pieces I remembered having a problem lining up the holes in the battery with the adapter. With all the finesse of a bull in the china shop I jammed it together and moved on. I had lined up the holes backwards. This was a very costly mistake; they don't give these batteries away. On the plus side, I now know how to make a bomb out of an Excaliber battery.

* * * * *

My mom would always say things like, "You can't squeeze blood out of a turnip." I was a very confused young lad.

Many years ago I purchased a Minelab Sovereign from Phil Alexander at Common Cents Metal Detectors and was having a great time with it. The first two times out I'd found over five dollars in change each time and was having my way with the beach. It was remarkable how easy it was. Simply turn on the machine, swing a few times, and then dig the targets.

I planned my assault on Myrtle Beach. Fourth of July weekend I would camp out at Apache Campground and rake in the dough and maybe some gold rings just to make things interesting.

Apache Campground informed me that all the camping spots were taken but that I could set up my little backpack tent on the lawn out front. Maybe I should have made reservations. OK, no problem.

It was firecracker hot. As I started my way down the beach I wondered if the detector was broken. I wasn't getting any signals. I checked the detector by swinging close to an empty chaise lounge chair. After the ringing in my ears stopped I surmised that the detector was fine.

In the first hour of intense sweating I found one dime. *It can't be this hot.* In the second hour I added a couple of pennies. *This is cruel and unusual punishment.* In the third hour I found a dime, a nickel, and another penny. I mumbled something about a death march. I pulled out my cell phone and called Phil. After I explained who I was I asked, "What's going on? I can't find anything."

"The beach is probably sanded-in."

"Sanded-in?"

"Yeah, the beach gets sanded-in and then you can't find anything."

"There's fourteen million people on the beach."

"Yeah, but the beach is sanded-in."

"But there's fourteen million people on the beach."

I thought I heard a chuckle. "Yeah, but the beach is sanded-in. The sand has covered up everything except what has been lost in the last fifteen minutes."

I ended up finding twenty eight cents in the hottest four hours of my life.

As I lay awake all night in my sweltering hot backpack tent I heard voices, first was Phil's voice that echoed "sanded-in, sanded-in, sanded-in" and then a tiny voice from the past, "You can't squeeze blood out of a turnip.

Never Take Your Gold to a Pawn Shop!

A few years ago I found what I thought was a gold ring, however it was not marked. I told Vince, "Let's stop in at Bob's (not the real name) Pawn Shop and have them check it.

After the pawn shop guy verified that it was 10K I asked, "Just for the sake of knowing, what would you give me for that ring?"

He replied, "Fifteen dollars."

I remember the ring as being a middle-weight ring, maybe close to five or six grams.

Even then that ring would have been worth at least $75 if I would have sent it to the refineries.

Also, a few years ago I found a nice starburst gold ring, 14K with one diamond in the center and six diamonds surrounding it. I really liked this ring. It is one of the few rings that have diamonds that really looked masculine. I had it appraised at over $1000 retail.

I decided to stop by the local pawn shop and see what I would be offered.

The pawn shop owner said, "I sold one just like that last week for $100."

I walked out of there angry. What are the chances that the pawn shop had another gold starburst ring and just sold it?"

I was not going to write this chapter. I didn't feel that I had enough expertise with selling gold.

Don Lewis, good friend and mystery writer, and I were having lunch. He said that a couple that his wife knew were having financial struggles and had sold their gold to a pawn shop for $4800.

I went ballistic!!! "I would have given them $6000, sight unseen. A pawn shop is the last place I would take my gold!"

I went undercover. I took a plain 10K 5.8 gram gold wedding band to twelve different places in Myrtle Beach that buy gold. Six were pawn shops, three were jewelry stores, and three were Cash for Gold type places.

The amount that a pawn shop would pay for the ring varied from:

1. "I think the ring is a fake. I couldn't get it to test 10K. The melt value is probably worth $35-$40."
2. $65
3. $65
4. $70
5. $80
6. $85

The jewelry stores would pay:

1. $78
2. $80
3. $90

The Cash for Gold places would pay:

1. $30   This very nice looking woman was very personable and bent forward to show her cleavage as she got out some paperwork. "What did you need to get for the ring?"

"I don't have any idea," I said.

After she weighed it and did some calculations she said, "I could give you thirty dollars."

I grabbed my ring and ran out the door.

2. $66.

3. $80

Let's do the math to determine what we could get for the ring from a refinery. The refinery I will be using in the example pays 98% of spot value for the day.

(www.Aragold.com)

Things we need to know:

Gold is measured in troy ounces. A troy ounce is 31.1 grams.

We need to know the spot value of gold. The spot value for today is $1812.50 per ounce or $58.28 per gram. ($1812.50 divided by 31.1).

The gold wedding band is 10K or 41.67% gold (the rest is alloy). 41.67% times 5.8 grams (the weight of the ring) is 2.417 grams of pure gold.

2.417 X $58.28 = $140.86

For this example the refinery will pay you 98% of spot value.

.98 X $140.86 = $138.04

The gold ring's scrap value, if sent to a refinery, is $138.

To be honest, I was very surprised that the one jewelry store in the mall would pay $90 for the ring. As you can see, there were many places that wanted to pay less than half of the value of the gold. There were also two places that wanted to blatantly rip me a new one.

My experiences with selling gold to a refinery have been positive for the most part. Knowledge of what carat the gold is and how much it weighs helps level out the playing field. A magnifying glass and a small scale (Jennings JS-150V) are the tools I use to determine what a piece of gold is worth.

I do not recommend any specific refinery. Reputations and service have a way of changing with time. Before you sell your gold you might want to ask the detectorists on the forums for their input.

One last thought. A couple of years ago I sold some gold to a refinery when the price was $800 an ounce. At the time I was overjoyed by the price. Now, it is consistently over $1600 per ounce.

• Never, ever take your gold to a pawn shop!

The Return

What is a gold ring? What emotions are hidden in the heavy metal that fits upon the finger?

Standing at a display case and picking out a gold ring to give to someone is a heavy emotional trip. Will they like it? Am I doing the right thing? Her fingers are kind of pudgy; I wonder what size she wears? How are guys supposed to know all this stuff? Maybe I should have Googled, "Buying a diamond ring," before I came in here."

And then there is the love factor. This ring is a symbol of that love, a symbol for life, the ultimate outward expression of love.

And when that gold ring is lost in the sand or in the waves it is as if one has been punched in the stomach. Memories of the proposal, the wedding, the happiness, the giddiness of fresh love flash across the mind; a part of all of that is now lost. How many men and women have fallen to their knees and dug the sand with their hands hoping to catch a glimpse of their golden past? How many tears have fallen upon the sand?

This is part of a post I put on Surf and Sand forum. September 20, 2011

I work down to my secret spot and pick up quite a few coins and then move further south. A young man with a worried face asks me if I could help find his wife's wedding band. They have a six foot wide hole dug, filled with water, and the band has slipped into the shells and sand. Four swings and I get a signal. I scoop and spread the sand on the damp beach.

The young lady, maybe eighteen or so, says, "Oh, I hope you can find it."

I spot a ring in the pile of sand and reach down, "Does it look like this one?"

Her face beams. I hand it to her. The couple hugs each other.

The titanium ring is a real nice design with a cross on it.

I feel like I have a big S on my chest. They thank me and off I go. I don't exactly fly because I've been swinging for three hours.

The return to the starting point is a few coins. I dig a couple more coins where I came onto the beach and then head for the house. Great Morning!

A Thousand Mornings

A thin band of low clouds lie at the horizon as they so often do just before the dawn. To the north, finger wisp clouds reach up to grab hold of the dark blue. Seagulls line the shore and a small flock of dark pigeons huddle close together higher on the beach. A solid warm breeze pushes the seawater and the waves run south to north looking as though they are traveling, going somewhere, in a hurry.

The gulls walk about nervously as the sky lightens, some take to the air.

They are not flying anywhere, just flying, flying, leaning right and then left and circling, dark against the burgeoning heavens. More take off from the beach, a hundred gulls whirling as if in an eddy, dodging each other.

At the rim of the world where the silver water and sky meet, the edge of a nickel rises out of the sea. I have made it to another day and I cheer inside.

The orb ascends; the transformation subtle but quick, melting from gray white, to whitish yellow, to yellow-orange, from weakness to strength.

The ocean holds tight to the fiery blob, elongating the sun, not letting go. For an instant the red marble is pulled into an hourglass of flame, half in the sky, half on the sea. The molten hourglass stretches in the middle until at last the thin red bond is shredded and the sun is set free.

I remember where I am and I take a breath. The beach is mine. I give thanks for another day.

I have been blessed with a life filled with beauty; too many images to count. I've seen the green and blue moving curtains of the aurora borealis in the snow covered wilderness of Alaska. While lying in my mummy sleeping bag on a mountain in the Colorado Rockies I've gazed at the swath of the Milky Way across the night sky where stars were so clear and close I knew I could reach up and touch them. I could go on and on. I love this earth. I love the beach.

It hurts to see the Sunday morning beach and the trash. The Saturday night trash people have left their cans, chaise lounge chairs, fishing poles, plastic bottles, towels, clothes, fast food boxes, chicken bones, plastic bags, and condoms.

Some trashy people find it perfectly acceptable to leave trash on the beach.

I've seen people wade into the surf with a bottle of beer and return to the beach empty handed. Many times I've seen people throw their cigarette butts on the beach.

Why would anyone want to ruin this world? What would be the motivation to defile a beautiful place? It makes no sense. The person that throws trash on the beach is brain damaged, plain and simple. There is no possible way that a clear thinking individual would want to make something beautiful into something ugly.

We have an opportunity to make things better, not just leave them as we found them. Better, not the same, better.

Very few things piss me off worse than when a beach detectorist leaves an open hole with a trash target (pull tab, bottle cap) lying next to it.

It does not take a genius to figure out that if they leave a pull tab or bottle cap on the beach that there is a chance down the road that they will have to dig it up again.

There are good people in the world and bad people in the world. There are people who care about our world and people who don't give a rat's ass. It's an attitude.

It has been said that if you are not part of the solution you are part of the problem.

Fill your holes and pick up your trash. If you have room in your pouch, pick up one piece of trash left by the trashy, brain damaged people. Do this every time you're on the beach and you have made things better. Better, not the same, better.

Summary

Finding Gold is Not Luck.

Know your detector and make it ergonomic.

Move away from renourished beaches. Do not torture mole crabs.

Use Run and Gun to Find the Erosion and the Gold.

Learn to read the beach to see the opportunities.

Be brutally honest about your assessment of the beach and surf.

Think about the clues from what you are digging; lightweight vs. heavyweight targets.

Fist-sized rock and conch shells are the #1 clue as to where the gold is hidden.

Green coins and sinkers are excellent clues to where the gold is located.

Are you detecting the hard layer; shell layer, peat layer, hardpan, or dark gray sand where the gold is?

Don't bend over to pick up that target!! Use your scoop or shovel. Save your back!

When you have too many targets, discriminate and get the gold.

There should be a sense of urgency to your hunt. That hole or runnel may not be there next low tide. Do it now!

Workable conditions. Sometimes you only have one hour at dead low tide to work a hole. Seize the moment!

Go fast. Run Forrest, Run. Go slow, really critique the eroded area!

New drops do not exist!! Hammer this home. You are looking for Erosion!!

Bad thinking; is intermittent reinforcement ruining your life?

Summer is usually the worst season to look for gold at MB.

Winds coming straight into the beach sand-in the beach. Winds at an acute angle to the beach erode the beach. Winds from the shore toward the ocean knock down the waves and make the surf workable.

Chase the storms

Hateful weather is good.

The Extra Low tides do not exist in the afternoons.

Keep a journal or photo record of your gold finds. Use it to understand what worked.

Analyze your bad days. Why didn't you find the gold? Failure is good.

Do not pre-judge a beach. Be open minded. Forget yesterday's success. Stay in the moment.

Use pilings and storm drains to determine how much sand is on the beach

Helping someone find a ring or their car keys will make you feel extraordinarily good. What goes around comes around.

If you choose to expedite the beach erosion with dynamite, do it on the 4th of July or New Years Eve. Try to blend in the explosions with the fireworks. Email me and let me know where you're doing this.

Enjoy the sunrise. You are blessed.

Real Treasure

It is boyish enthusiasm to think that one can find treasure. I feel true sorrow for those people who no longer think that magic can happen. How sad to go through life without the laughter of spirit, the joy of the hunt, and to see the sun rise out over the ocean, the pale sky filled with dark blue battleships.

In the summertime I get asked two or three times a day about detecting the beach by those that are curious. Children will rush up, "What'd you find, what'd you find?"

There are those who say to themselves, "What a waste of time." The struggle for money makes many see life as a dollar bill. If it doesn't bring in the money it's a waste of time. I had an Asian couple ask me about detecting. The man was only interested in how much money I made, the bottom line.

Many times my bottom line is less than a dollar in change.

In another time and place I would have been a gold miner, pulling a burro named Bad Dog, off into the sage covered mountains to hunt gold nuggets and dust. I probably would have been good at finding dust.

Those must have been grand times; to be all hunkered over at the streams edge, swirling the pieces of sunlight in a gold pan. It would have been tough to be all hunkered over all day but getting unhunkered, standing upright, and getting the knees to unlock from the hunkered position would have been worse. It may have been easier to just lean forward and fall into the stream.

I love the outdoors and hunting, always have and always will. I hope I die watching the sun rise or set, the wind in my face, the smell of earth or sea in my nostrils. For me, each day should include a hunt, a traipse in the world beyond walls and windows, a search for something.

The pelicans glide down the swell troughs on good days and flap big wings on bad days. We hunt erosion and gold rings and some days, when conditions are right, we unearth the treasure. For a short and glorious time we are as efficient as the gliding pelicans in the rolling swells.

Links

Metal Detecting Forums

www.thetreasuredepot.com
www.findmall.com

Tide Charts

www.saltwatertides.com

Weather

www.weatherchannel.com
http://www.wunderground.com/MAR/AM/254.html

Surf Cams

http://www.bar-harbor.com/webcam.html
http://www.beachtrips.com/webcam.cfm
http://www.daytonhouse.com/landing/dayton-house-web-cam/
http://www.funbeaches.com/beach_cams-new.html

The websites offering surf cams seem to change fairly often, so this may not be current. You may have to Google to get a surf cam of your beach.

Surf Report...very interesting website

http://www.swellinfo.com/surf-forecast/myrtle-beach-south-carolina.html

YouTube of me in the surf

http://www.youtube.com/watch?v=Ktg6SwSPaMc

Excellent Video on the Sov. GT

http://www.mlotv.com/view/843/the-sovereign-gt-de-mystified/

Detector Dealers

Common Cents Metal Detectors   910 471 2457

Accessories

www.sunraydetector.com
www.detectorpro.com
www.metaldetecting.com
Sunspot Scoops
http://www.gold-scoop.com/thescoop.html

Clive Clynick's Website

http://clivesgoldpage.com

Myrtle Beach Shore Protection Program

http://www.sac.usace.army.mil/?action=programs.myrtle_
beach

Index

Made in the USA
Middletown, DE
25 March 2016